WORKERS' HOUSING IN WEST YORKSHIRE, 1750–1920

PUBLICATIONS IN THE SUPPLEMENTARY SERIES OF THE
ROYAL COMMISSION ON THE HISTORICAL MONUMENTS OF ENGLAND:

1. Liverpool Road Station, Manchester: an historical and architectural survey
(Manchester University Press, 1980)

2. Northamptonshire: an archaeological atlas (RCHM, 1980)

3. Early Industrial Housing: the Trinity area of Frome (HMSO, 1981)

4. Beverley: an archaeological and architectural study (HMSO, 1982)

5. Pottery Kilns of Roman Britain (HMSO, 1984)

6. Danebury: An Iron Age Hill Fort (RCHM, 1984)

7. Liverpool's Historic Waterfront (HMSO, 1986)

8. Rural Houses of West Yorkshire 1400–1830 (HMSO, 1984)

10. Rural Houses of the Lancashire Pennines 1560–1760 (HMSO, 1985)

This publication has been assisted by a grant from West Yorkshire Metropolitan County Council.

WEST YORKSHIRE METROPOLITAN COUNTY COUNCIL

ROYAL COMMISSION ON THE HISTORICAL MONUMENTS
OF ENGLAND

Supplementary Series: 9

Workers' Housing in West Yorkshire, 1750–1920

Lucy Caffyn

LONDON · HER MAJESTY'S STATIONERY OFFICE

© Crown copyright 1986
First published 1986

ISBN 0 11 300002 2

Printed for Her Majesty's Stationery Office by The Bath Press, Avon.   Dd 736290 C20 1/86

TABLE OF CONTENTS

LIST OF ILLUSTRATIONS

FIGURES

PLATES

MAP

SOURCES OF THE ILLUSTRATIONS

Fig. 8, R. Thornes; Fig. 25, M.W. Beresford; Figs 26, 48, 59, 60 are based on O.S. plans; Pl. 1, British Waterways Board; Pls 3, 52, 79–82, 106–111, 115, Leeds City Libraries; Pls 133, 134, Royal Institute of British Architects; Pls 150–155, Bradford Metropolitan Libraries; Pls 172–5, National Monuments Record. The above mentioned illustrations are reproduced by permission of the persons or bodies acknowledged. Other plates are from RCHM photographs and the plans were drawn for this survey in the West Yorkshire Metropolitan Archaeology Unit's drawing office.

PREFACE

The value of studying workers' housing is becoming ever more widely recognized, while the degree of physical threat to which such housing is exposed makes the need to examine and record it increasingly urgent. In West Yorkshire the County Council and the Royal Commission on Historical Monuments have recognized this need and joined forces to make a positive contribution to the subject by financing this survey. A previous joint venture (RCHM forthcoming) examined the rural housing of the county from 1400 to the early 19th century. The object of the present project was to examine the housing of less affluent people, further down the social scale, and to continue the story into the 20th century. The period studied was one of great change and development in the county, and developments in the field of housing are seen to be a reflection of changes which occurred in the county's social and economic structure.

The survey was carried out over a period of two years by Lucy Caffyn (Mrs. L. Dewhurst), assisted by the Royal Commission's photographers and for six months by an illustrator. Housing throughout the county was visited and recorded, further information being supplied by research into primary and secondary sources. Records of the results are held in the Sites and Monuments Record, County Archaeology Unit, County Hall, Wakefield, West Yorkshire, and in the National Monuments Record, Fortress House, 23 Savile Row, London.

It is hoped that this publication, although by no means definitive, will show the value of a joint historical and architectural approach in this field and will be of interest and value not only to students of local history and architecture but also to planners, conservationists and architects. The Commissioners and the members of the County Council wish to express their thanks to all concerned in the production of this volume, in particular to the owners and occupiers of the houses recorded. Finally, this work is another example of successful co-operation; the Royal Commission and the County Council have combined fruitfully to produce a work which covers an important aspect of the architectural environment. Its initiation and completion within a short period is largely due to the scope offered by shared resources, and it is hoped that other gaps in our knowledge can be filled by similar joint projects.

JOHN M. SULLY
Chairman, Recreation and Arts Committee,
West Yorkshire Metropolitan
County Council

P. J. FOWLER
Secretary, Royal Commission on the
Historical Monuments of England

EDITORIAL NOTES

The numbers in brackets throughout the text refer to the inventory where the full addresses and map references of buildings discussed can be found. The house plans have been drawn to show as far as possible the original arrangements of each, omitting modern additions. In a row of houses only one unit has been drawn fully, although the fireplaces and external walls of neighbouring units have been shown to indicate their positions. In those houses where cellars have been infilled or where roofs were inaccessible these features have been omitted from the plan or section, although their presence has been indicated. The plans have been arranged so that in each case the front door faces the foot of the page. Where plans show more than one floor, the lower floors are to the left or below the upper floors.

THE FOLLOWING CONVENTIONS HAVE BEEN USED IN THE PLANS

B	Bath	⌐	Privy, Earth Closet or Water closet
C	Wall Cupboard	▨	Coal Hole
K	Sink	▨	Infilled Opening
S	Stone Ledge or Table	▨	Set-pot

ACKNOWLEDGEMENTS

Many people have been involved in this survey; without their help and co-operation the work would have moved more slowly and have been less productive. In particular I would like to thank Robin Thornes of the Royal Commission on Historical Monuments (England) who initiated the project and has always been ready to offer help and advice, which has been especially valuable in the initial and final stages. His colleague, Colum Giles, who has been working on the parallel survey of rural houses, has also been a ready source of valuable assistance and criticism. David Michelmore, formerly of the County Archaeology Unit, has likewise supplied information and offered comments on the text.

Also essential to the progress of the survey have been all those householders who have given me their co-operation and assistance and have supplied additional information. I am indebted to many others who have made available their own research and specialist knowledge, including especially H. Bamforth, Professor M. Beresford, J. Goodchild, D. Nortcliffe, G. Redmonds, P. Round, A. Saul, G. Sheeran, Mrs R. Strong, and T. Wainright.

My own research was facilitated by the assistance which I received from the Local Studies Department, Bradford Metropolitan Libraries; the Brotherton Library, University of Leeds; the Halifax Building Society; Kirklees Council Planning Services; the Local Studies Department, Kirklees Libraries and Art Galleries; Leeds City Libraries; the Leeds Permanent Building Society; the City of Wakefield Metropolitan District Council Planning Department; and West Yorkshire Archive Service at Bradford, Calderdale, Leeds and Wakefield.

I am grateful for the permission to reproduce material used in this book given by the Bradford Metropolitan Libraries; the British Waterways Board; J. Goodchild; Leeds City Libraries; and the Royal Institute of British Architects.

Finally I would like to thank the staff of the County Archaeology Unit's drawing office, in particular P. Hudson, who produced most of the published drawings, and A. Swan, who completed the work, and all those who have been involved in the final stages of producing this book.

LUCY CAFFYN

WORKERS' HOUSING IN WEST YORKSHIRE 1750–1920

INTRODUCTION

The functional appearance and uniformity of much workers' housing, which has deterred so many historians from examining it, in fact conceals a large number of types, varying widely both in design and construction. Between the rural labourers' cottages of the 18th century and the council estates of the inter-war years in the 20th century came a number of important intermediate stages, each a reflection of the social and economic changes which were occurring in society as a whole. These changes are most immediately apparent in the mechanisms by which housing was provided, in the size of developments, and in the standard of accommodation. This transformation, which began in the late 18th century with the building of workers' housing on an unprecedented scale, poses a number of questions. Foremost among these are: who provided the housing? why was it provided? and why did it take the particular forms that it did?

The growing number of workers' houses and the increasing size and sophistication of individual dwellings required capital investment on a previously unparalleled scale. Comprehension of the various ways in which such capital was raised is important to our understanding of the subject as a whole. Another factor of increasing importance, particularly in the later half of the period, was that of governmental intervention, both at local and at national levels.

This survey is confined to the modern metropolitan county of West Yorkshire, an area which by the early 19th century had already become one of the country's principal manufacturing districts. The industrial expansion of the county, based largely on textiles, coal and iron, created a new landscape, in which an important element was the housing built for the workforce of those industries. The houses examined have been restricted to the dwellings occupied by those strata of society, from the unskilled labourer to the skilled artisan, which by the 1830s were being referred to by contemporaries as the working classes. It is not always easy to determine whether a particular individual or house falls within this category, making it difficult to draw fine distinctions in the grey area at the upper end of the working class and the lower end of the middle class.

Time and resources, as well as the vast amount of surviving housing, have precluded any attempt at a definitive study. It has rather been the aim to trace the principal trends, to detail the major house types of the period, and a number of minor types, and to explain their development by placing them in a wider historical context. The survey has examined housing ranging in date from the mid 18th century to the 1920s. Relatively few examples of workers' houses survive prior to the earlier date, while the latter marks the beginning, both technologically and conceptually, of a new era in the history of workers' housing.

MAP: West Yorkshire: principal places mentioned in text (Model villages underlined)

CHAPTER 1

HOUSING AND INDUSTRY IN THE LATE 18TH CENTURY

The major problem which faces any study of the historical development of workers' housing is the paucity of surviving examples prior to the second half of the 18th century. There are a number of reasons which account for this, foremost amongst these being the fact that successive generations have had differing perceptions as to what constituted the acceptable minimum standard of accommodation. Housing regarded as adequate in a particular period was not necessarily still so regarded in subsequent ones. This factor, when taken in combination with those of physical decay and relatively poor construction, has meant that such dwellings have either been demolished or altered beyond all recognition.

In the absence of surviving examples knowledge of such cottages must, to a large extent, be based on documentary sources and the accounts of contemporary observers. From these it is evident that the traditional form of accommodation for the majority of the labouring-classes in pre-industrial West Yorkshire was the single-storey cottage. The evidence of probate inventories indicates that the landless or low-income labourers, and some more wealthy, lived in single-storey cottages comprising one or two rooms (a 'house-body' and a 'parlour').[1] Early maps also show the predominance of this type of dwelling. Seventeenth-century maps of Almondbury, Baildon Common and Silsden depict some two-storey houses, but the majority are of only one storey.

A plan of the Aire and Calder Navigation, made in 1775, again indicates a larger number of single-storey than of two-storey cottages (Pl 1) (Commissioners' Plan 1775). A deed of 1707 describes one such cottage, probably typical of many:

> Wee, whos names are unto subscribed doo freely give our consent without let or hinderance unto Paull Ellis, of Morley, to build, for himself his wife and children, one little Cottighouse of six yards in lengt, and four yards in breadtg, upon a certain parcell of Wast ground, Comanly called the name of Lower Sinder Hill, which may be best for his own convenience and the least pregedis for his Neighbours, and hereunto wee have set to our hands this sixth day of March, 1707 . . . (Smith 1866, 183).

From examples surviving in the early 19th century, the Morley historian Norrison Scatcherd concluded that such early cottages 'appear to have been single apartments without chambers – open to their thatched roofs – and supported upon crooks [crucks] – without chimneys – without pavement – low, confined, dark, and comfortless'. The fact that some cottages were built in this manner, and often no more solidly than 'of lath and plaster' (Scatcherd 1874, 132, 147), explains why no obvious physical record of them survives. Nineteenth-century illustrations of single-

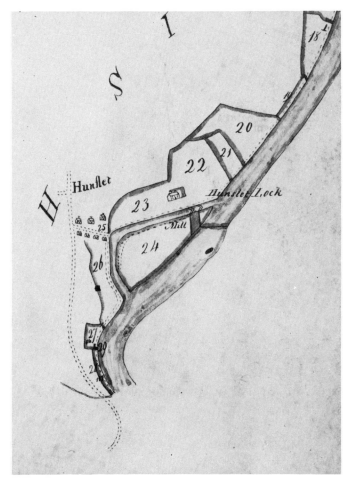

Plate 1. Detail from the Aire and Calder Navigation plan, 1775

Plate 2. Single-storey cottages, Town Quarry, Morley

Plate 3. Single-storey cottage, Adel

Plate 4. Cottages, Ratten Row, Lepton

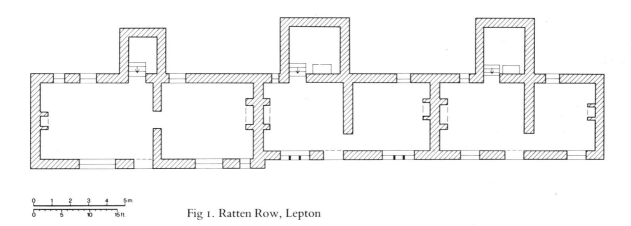

0 1 2 3 4 5 m.
0 5 10 15 ft.

Fig 1. Ratten Row, Lepton

storey cottages show them to have been low stone structures, often with thatched roofs (Pls 2, 3). Those which
survive, however, generally had a roof covering of stone
slates supported on roughly-shaped oak timbers.

The simplest and smallest type of single-storey cottage to
be found is that which consists of one room only, this
having to serve as kitchen, living-room, workroom and
bedroom. Cottages of this type have often been enlarged at a
later date, although unaltered examples survive. When a
dwelling was provided with a second room this was
generally built alongside the living-room, as in Ratten Row,
Lepton (74) (Pl 4, Fig 1). Alternatively, it could be built
behind the living-room, as was done at Waterloo Fold,
Wyke (158), a slightly later example built in the early 19th
century (Fig 2). A further way of increasing the accom-

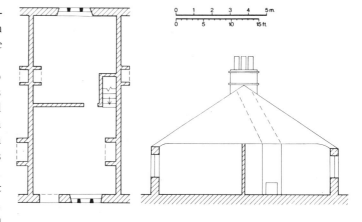

0 1 2 3 4 5 m.
0 5 10 15 ft.

Fig 2. No. 2, Waterloo Fold, Wyke

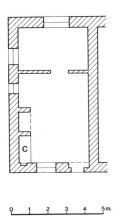

Fig 3.
No.10, School Fold, Low Moor

modation was to build a small pantry outshut for food storage (see Fig 6). In some houses this outshut was extended the full length of the building, as in the mid-18th-century cottages in School Fold, Low Moor (100) (Fig 3). Another means of creating additional food storage space was to provide a cellar, but these tend not to be found as an original feature before the second decade of the 19th century and then only occasionally. The cottage in Waterloo Fold (158), which dates to that period, was built with cellars, as were those at Hudd Hill, Shelf (c.1835) (Fig 4).

In some parts of Britain 'cocklofts' or 'crogglofts' were used to provide more sleeping and storage room in single-storey cottages.[2] The cockloft was a platform created simply by laying timbers across the width of the cottage from wall to wall upon which boards were rested. There are very few examples of cocklofts in West Yorkshire, although since they could be removed leaving little trace it may be

that they were once common. An example of such a loft survives in one of three cottages created by the subdivision of a barn at Rodwell End, Stansfield (Pls 5, 6; Fig 5).

The cottages at Rodwell End (131), situated in an isolated group with a large yeoman's house and other farm buildings, were probably occupied by farm workers. For much of the 18th century, however, there is little evidence of agricultural labourers' accommodation, since this class of worker frequently lived in their employers' houses or outbuildings. As late as 1843 work on the graziers' farms in the Yorkshire Dales was carried out by 'house-servants', that is, living-in agricultural workers (Kussmaul 1981, 6). Some fifty years earlier Robert Brown, in describing the agriculture of the West Riding of Yorkshire, observed that 'almost the whole of the farm servants are young unmarried men, who have board in the house, while those that are styled day-labourers reside in the village' (Brown 1799, 13). The day-labourers would, for the most part, have been those workers who had moved out of the house when they

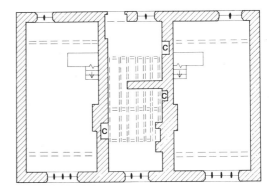

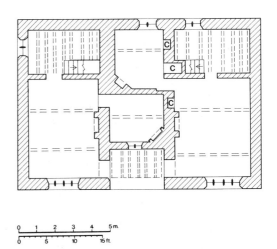

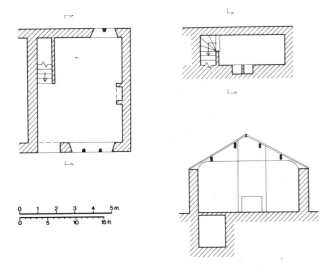

Fig 4. No.17, Hudd Hill, Shelf

Fig 5. Converted barn, Rodwell End, Stansfield

Plate 5 (*above*).
Converted barn,
Rodwell End,
Stansfield

Plate 6 (*left*).
Barn, Rodwell End,
rear view

Plate 7.
Nos. 17 and 19,
Station Road,
Cullingworth

got married and, as far as accommodation was concerned, had to fend for themselves. Farmers do not, on the whole, seem to have supplied tied cottages, for not only was it cheaper for them to employ labour on a casual basis, but also such were the mechanisms of the poor-law legislation that 'the farmer, from a dread of heavier rates falling upon him, keeps as few houses as possible' (Brown 1799, 13), the result being 'a great want of dwelling houses for husbandmen and labourers' (Ibid). Brown recommended 'that proper houses should be built for farm servants, contiguous to every homestead' giving his reasons for this approach as being that:

> This will not only promote the welfare and happiness of that class of men, by giving them an opportunity of settling in life, which is not at present an easy matter, but will also be highly beneficial to the farmer himself, as he will at all times have people within his own bounds, for carrying on his labour; and have them of that description, that are generally esteemed most regular and careful (Ibid 13–14).

There is evidence that, in the absence of purpose-built cottages, farm labourers lived in converted farmhouses and outbuildings. Accommodation of this type appears to have

been most common in the western half of the county. Numbers 17 and 19 Station Road, Cullingworth (9) (Pl 7), are the result of an 18th-century division of an earlier farmhouse, each cottage containing a living-room and scullery on the ground floor with two bedrooms above (one of these being heated). The three cottages at Rodwell End are the products of an ingenious conversion, also dating to this period (mid 18th century) comprising a pair of two-storeyed cottages and a third of one storey (Fig 5).

From the second half of the 18th century there are surviving examples of squatters' cottages built on common and waste land. The men who built these cottages were mentioned in manorial court records on occasion (RCHM forthcoming; Sheeran 1984; Stell 1960). One such entry, in 1775, records that Ake Akroyd enclosed half an acre of waste land in Thornton. The cottage shown in Pl 8, Fig 6 and built on the site in the late 18th century is likely to have superseded an earlier, less substantial, squatter's cottage. Other similar cottages sited haphazardly on roadsides and commons are often found in mining areas and are likely to have been built on land similarly encroached upon.

In the early 18th century the population of the west of the county was growing considerably more rapidly than in the east. In 1726, for example, it was estimated that over the previous forty years the population of the large upland

Plate 8. Squatter's cottage, Half Acre Lane, Thornton

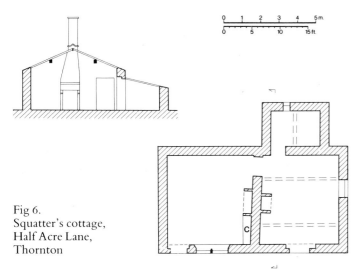

Fig 6.
Squatter's cottage,
Half Acre Lane,
Thornton

parish of Halifax had quadrupled (Defoe 1971, 495). As the population grew, so too did the need to accommodate it. On his journey across the Pennines from Lancashire into Yorkshire in that year, Daniel Defoe noted the dense, though dispersed, settlement of the area:

> The nearer we came to Hallifax, we found the houses thicker, and the villages greater in every bottom; and not only so, but the sides of the hills, which were very steep every way, were spread with houses, and that very thick; for the land being divided into small enclosures . . . every three or four pieces of land had a house belonging to it (Ibid 491).

This increase in population was largely brought about by the expansion of the county's wool textile industry. From the late Middle Ages onwards this had become concentrated increasingly in the valleys of the Pennines, thus resulting in the pattern of settlement observed by Defoe. In the early 18th century the industry was dominated by the yeoman-clothiers, below whom in its hierarchy came the weavers and other miscellaneous textile workers, the majority working either in the houses of clothiers' or in their own homes. Defoe noticed amongst the larger houses 'an infinite number of cottages or small dwellings, in which dwelt the workmen which are employed' (Defoe 1971, 493). Some of these may have been single-storey cottages, for there is evidence from the 19th century that textile workers were still living in accommodation of that type.[3]

The growth of the textile industry in the last quarter of the 18th century stimulated an expansion of the economy of the area as a whole, this, in turn, having a considerable impact on the towns. Of the towns which existed in West Yorkshire in the 18th century, some, like Bradford, Leeds, Pontefract and Wakefield, had been granted borough status in the Middle Ages. These subsequently expanded as marketing, manufacturing, and, in the cases of Pontefract and Wakefield, administrative centres. As a commercial centre Leeds attained a predominant position, by the 1690s being 'esteemed the wealthyest town of its bigness in the Country, its manufacture is the woollen cloth the Yorkshire Cloth in which they are all employ'd' (Morris 1947, 219). New concentrations of population were brought into

Plate 9. Booth's Yard, Pudsey

Fig 7. Booth's Yard, Pudsey

existence in the 16th and 17th centuries, most as a direct result of the expansion of the domestic textile industry and the growing demand for more localized marketing centres.

For much of the 18th century it was possible to house town-dwellers within the original urban boundaries by building up existing areas of housing. As vacant plots along street frontages were occupied the tenements and yards running back behind them tended to be built-up in a process which accentuated the pattern of linear property division persisting in the layout of the larger medieval towns (Beresford 1974, 282). In Booths Yard, Pudsey (106), the infill process began in the late 17th century with the construction of domestic and industrial building on either side of a narrow yard. The addition of other cottages in the 18th century completed the development (see Pl 9 and Fig 7). In the larger towns yard infilling was accelerated in the second half of the century by the trend for wealthier townsfolk to abandon congested town centres and remove to less crowded, more salubrious areas on the outskirts. This migration allowed their houses to be subdivided and the back-yards of these to be developed (Wilson 1971, 195, 203). Between 1767 and 1805 twenty-five cottages were built in Boot and Shoe Yard, Leeds, some at least of which consisted

of 'a Low Room and a Chamber, a Pantry, Cellar and Coalhouse', while others comprised a single room only (Beresford 1980, 75–76, fig 12; Rimmer 1963, 169). When another similarly developed yard situated off Boar Lane, Leeds, was sold in 1773 it contained three 'new' houses fronting the street and a dozen cottages in the yard behind (Wilson 1971, 196). From the documentary sources a picture emerges of the type of accommodation occupied by poorer urban dwellers, but, as with other types of workers' houses, little physical evidence survives before the late 18th century. Not only did the insubstantial nature of the cottages make them unlikely to survive, but in the towns, where building land was at a premium, there were also the additional threats of replacement by later dwellings or clearance to allow redevelopment.

[1] Borthwick Institute of Historical Research, York, Exchequer Probate Records: information taken from a sample of inventories from the Deanery of Pontefract used in the WYMCC post-medieval survey (Thornes 1981, 8–10) and in the RCHM architectural survey (RCHM forthcoming).
[2] Cocklofts were used, for example, in Wales (Lowe 1977, 10) and in southern England (*Builder* 1860, 803).
[3] In 1841 one of the occupants of Ratten Row, Lepton (74) was recorded as being a weaver (WYAS, Wakefield, Census 1841, Lepton).

CHAPTER 2

EXPANSION

THE TEXTILE INDUSTRY

The textile industry, already firmly established as the most important single industry in West Yorkshire, began to expand at an unprecedented rate in the 1780s (see Fig 8). This growth was made possible by a combination of an increased demand for cloth with developments in textile technology. Cloth fulling had been power-driven since the Middle Ages, but during the second half of the 18th century power was applied to certain other processes, the most important being scribbling, slubbing and spinning. The result of the mechanization of such processes was a considerable increase in yarn output which, in turn, made possible an expansion of the weaving sector.

One way in which employers created workspace for their weavers was by bringing them together under one roof in loomshops. Where accommodation was required for only a few weavers, the loomshop could be small and might occupy part of the employer's house or outbuildings. By the last quarter of the century clothiers' houses had begun to include recognizable upper-floor loomshops, as was the case in a house in the hamlet of Oldfield (55) (Pl 10) built in 1773. In addition to working space on the first floor this house had a second-floor workroom with a loft above for storage. Another clothier's house, at Ryecroft (19) (illustrated in

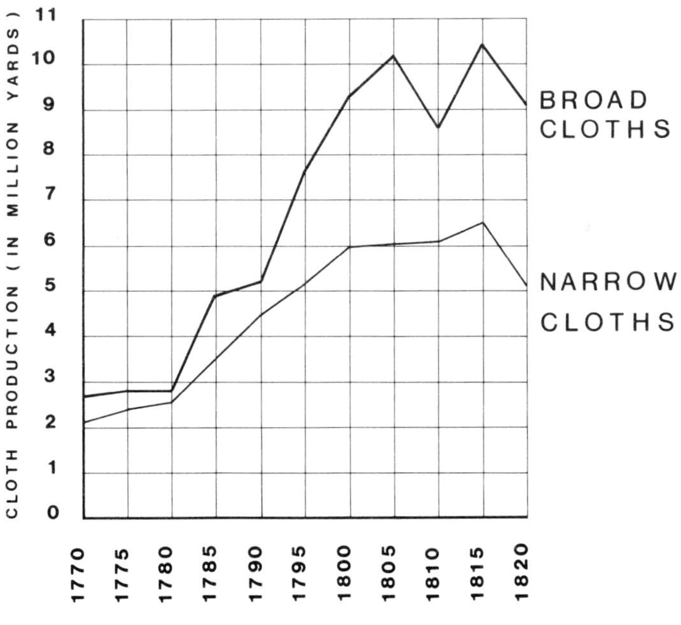

Fig 8. Cloth production in West Yorkshire, 1770–1820

Plate 10. No.28, Oldfield, Honley

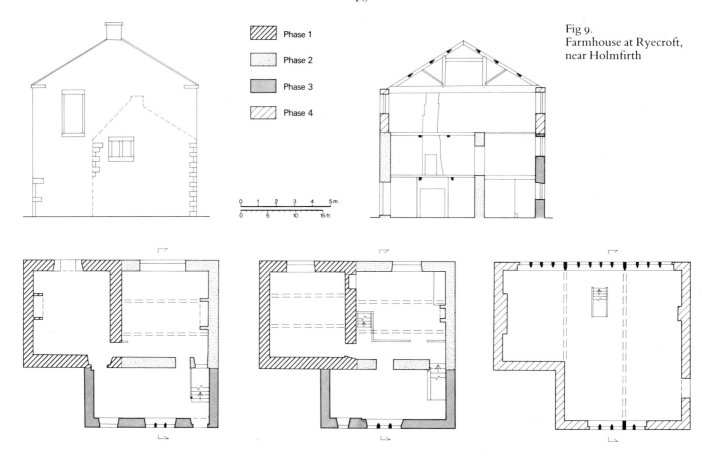

Phase 1	
Phase 2	
Phase 3	
Phase 4	

0 1 2 3 4 5 m.
0 5 10 15 ft.

Fig 9.
Farmhouse at Ryecroft,
near Holmfirth

Plate 11 (*left*).
Barn at Oldfield, Honley

Plate 12. Loomshop and cottages, The Rookery, Addingham

Figure 9), had a third-storey weaving-room added to it in the late 18th century. As well as possessing a long, south-facing window, providing the maximum amount of light, this loomshop had a taking-in door which allowed materials to be taken in and out easily and avoided the necessity of workers passing through the house. At Oldfield weavers worked not only in the second-floor loomshop of the clothier's house (55) but also in the upper part of the barn (Pl 11). A number of manufacturers erected larger, free-standing, purpose-built loomshops. One, at The Rookery, Addingham (3), was built adjoining a row of cottages but functioned as a separate loomshop (Pl 12). Another, at Sowerby Bridge, was built to a height of four storeys.

The alternative to working in loomshops was the more common practice of weavers working at looms in their own homes. A number of those that did so were self-employed, purchasing their own raw materials which they then worked up into cloth and marketed themselves (Brown, 1799, 77–8). Others worked for particular masters, who supplied them with yarn and collected the finished cloth. One practitioner of this putting-out system was William Helm, who established himself in the woollen industry in Raistrick in the early 19th century. Helm's sons carried on the business after his death, employing 130 domestic hand-loom weavers by the mid 19th century (Barke 1975, 93–4). The cottages in which such weavers would have lived have

survived in large numbers, the great majority dating from the late 18th and early 19th century.

By the middle of the 18th century clothiers' houses had begun to be built semi-detached, an early example being built at Oldfield, Honley (56) in 1742 (Pl 13). This pair of two-storeyed houses was built well, although the accommodation they offered was fairly basic – comprising a living-room, scullery and a well-lit first-floor chamber.

Plate 13. Nos. 32 and 33, Oldfield, Honley

Plate 14. No. 1, St. Mary's Court, Honley

Fig 10.
No. 1, St. Mary's Court,
Honley

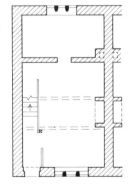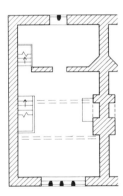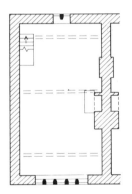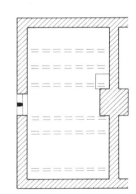

Also in Honley is a pair of larger, three-storeyed clothiers' houses, dating to the late 18th century (58) (Pl 14; Fig 10). These provided ample workshop accommodation both on the second floor and in a well-lit front room on the first floor. The attics, which were lit by gable-windows, would have provided an additional storage and sleeping area (attics are seldom found in housing of this type, upper floor loomshops being open to the roof usually) (Fig 12).

In building semi-detached houses economies were made in both land and materials. By the end of the 18th century it had become common practice to build houses in longer rows, so making even greater economies. Along Manchester Road, Linthwaite is a row of six such houses, each containing a third-storey workroom (Pls 15, 16; Fig 11). More common, however, was the two-storeyed weaver's cottage comprising a single room on each floor. From the evidence Joseph Coope of Pudsey gave to a parliamentary committee in 1806 it appears that one reason for building taller houses was the need for more weaving space – the mechanization of other previously domestic processes diverted those who had been engaged in them into weaving:

> while the slubbing was followed at home, it took the younger part of the family; they wrought in what we call the house-body; as we have not that work for the younger part of the family [it being moved to the slubbing mills], we put them to the loom at younger years than we did at that time. Consequently we want more upper rooms; airy rooms for the looms
> (Parliamentary Papers 1806, 45).

Many of the two-and-a-half and three-storeyed houses in Pudsey date to this period and they may be a reflection of the changes noted by Coope.

Both the two- and three-storeyed weavers' cottages often have distinctive features which reflect their original function. One of the most obvious of these was the provision of a large window area; since good lighting was an essential feature of a workroom. From the mid 18th century long, multi-light windows were provided, not only in the clothiers' houses and work-shops but also in small cottages; they are characteristic in the Colne, Holme and Calder Valleys.

Another indication of textile manufacture, found even at cottage level, is a door to an upper storey through which

Plate 15. Nos.437–445, Manchester Road, Linthwaite

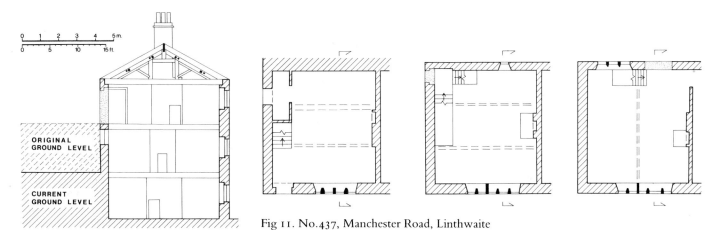

Fig 11. No.437, Manchester Road, Linthwaite

Plate 16 (*left*).
Nos. 437–445,
Manchester Road,
Linthwaite

Plate 17 (*below*).
Three-storeyed cottages
at New Longley, Norland

materials were taken to and from the workfloor. Sometimes there are steps up to the door, but more frequently there is no sign of these, in which case a ladder or hoist must have been used. Where there was no taking-in door, materials could be carried up the stairs and this was made easier by the provision next to them of a slide (a sloping board parallel to the stair). Another method was to raise and lower materials through a trap door in the floor of the workroom, as was done in 2 Green End, Old Town (148), for stairs were often no more than ladders and too narrow to allow bulky materials to be carried up and down with ease. Alternatively these could be taken in and out through the workroom windows. Many of the cottages situated in the steep-sided valleys were built back-to-earth, that is with their lower floor or floors backing onto the hillside. In these houses there would have been no difficulty in passing materials through the workroom windows, which at the back were at ground level. Use was also made of a higher ground level at the back in the siting of taking-in doors, as in 437 Manchester Road, Linthwaite (77), where, by siting the second-floor door at the back, it was positioned at ground level and no steps were needed (Pl 16). Taking-in doors and the lights of long windows were often blocked in at a later date when, with the decline in demand for domestic weaving, workrooms were turned over to purely domestic purposes. With this change in function doors and windows that were no longer necessary could be filled in to make the rooms warmer (see Pl 17). Blocked openings were not, however, always the result of later in-filling, some builders constructing their cottages with extra blocked-in windows

and taking-in doors with the intention that they could be unblocked as, or if, required.

There is evidence in some cottages of a shared workroom extending over two or more dwellings. An indication of such a workfloor is sometimes given by the provision of fewer taking-in doors in a terrace than there were cottages. As in the terrace at New Longley, Norland (94) (Pl 17) and in 437–445 Manchester Road, Linthwaite (77) (Fig 11), the shared workfloor was generally at an upper level, but in a few terraces like Long Row, Thornton (137), and Club

Plate 18
West Laithe, Heptonstall

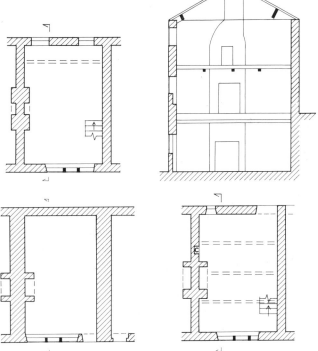

Fig 12. Nos. 9 and 12, West Laithe, Heptonstall

Row, Wilsden (155), it seems that the ground-floor rooms inter-communicated. From evidence such as the statement made by Joseph Coope (see p 13 above) it is known that work was done in the ground floor as well as the upper rooms and this may have given rise to a similar need for inter-communication. Sometimes the only means of access to the upper workfloor was through an exterior door; in such instances the domestic and industrial functions of the building were separated totally. This was the case with a pair of three-storeyed cottages in Golcar (Thornes 1981, 19, 21, 22) and on a larger scale in Coffin Row, Linthwaite where the second-floor workshop extended over four dwellings and was capable of holding forty looms (Bodey 1971, 388).

As well as the typical two and three-storeyed weavers' cottages, there are other dwellings which, although similar in appearance, were built to somewhat different designs. Often these were used to enable even denser development, particularly in the steep-sided valleys where there was a limited amount of flat building land available for cottage building. One of these variant plans was the dwelling-and-underdwelling by which, making use of the back-to-earth design, builders could construct a cottage with a separate dwelling beneath it, so producing two dwellings on a plot of land which would normally have allowed only one. The underdwelling was built back-to-earth and approached from the lower level, while the dwelling above it was reached from an upper road, or path, on the opposite side. Examples of this type of house survive in small numbers from the end of the 18th century. One example is at West Laithe,

Heptonstall (52) (Pl 18, Fig 12), a row of six dwellings and underdwellings, in which the underdwelling consists of a single barrel-vaulted room, with a two-storeyed dwelling above it. Another example in the same area is at Slaters Bank Farm, Hebden Bridge, where two underdwellings of the West Laithe type were constructed beneath a farmhouse.

Plate 19. Back-to-backs, Huddersfield Road, Thongsbridge

An alternative way of economizing on building land was to construct cottages back-to-back. In this method pairs of cottages were built backing on to each other sharing a common spine wall and under a single roof, so saving on building materials as well as on land. Back-to-backs survive

Plate 20. Datestone on back-to-backs, Huddersfield Road, Thongsbridge

from the late 18th century, one early dated example being a block of six built in 1790 on Huddersfield Road, Thongsbridge (90) (Pls 19, 20). Others occur throughout the textile area, in particular in the upper Calder Valley and in the Pudsey area. The same basic plan of a living-room with chamber over which was used in the two-storeyed weaver's cottage is found in the smallest back-to-backs, for example in a court of sixteen in Addingham (3) (Pl 21, Figs 13, 14). The back-to-back plan was also used for larger houses. Those in Northfield, Heptonstall (49), have an attic room and a scullery on the ground floor. In Pudsey there are several instances of two-and-a-half-storeyed back-to-backs, and the rear dwellings in the block of four on Gilroyd Lane, Linthwaite (76) are also large. Here the back houses each have three storeys, with a large living-room and scullery on the ground floor, several rooms on the first floor and a workroom on the second floor (Fig 15). Cottages like these, which provided more than the basic amount of accommodation, did not always require three floors to do so. In a terrace of twelve cottages in Burley-in-Wharfedale (16) comparable living and working space was provided on two floors by building each cottage on a larger ground area than was customary (Fig 28).

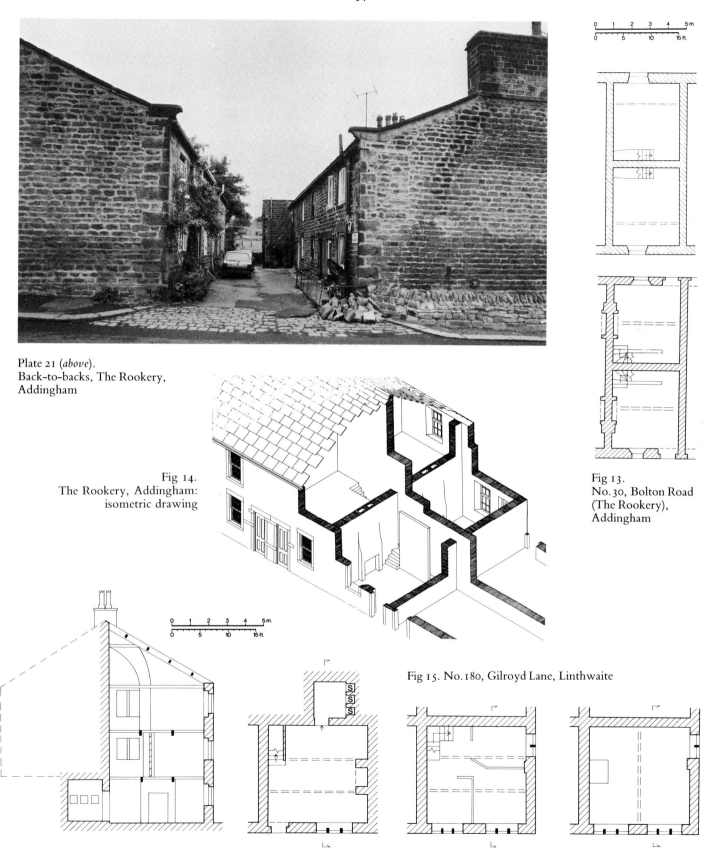

Plate 21 (*above*).
Back-to-backs, The Rookery,
Addingham

Fig 14.
The Rookery, Addingham:
isometric drawing

Fig 13.
No. 30, Bolton Road
(The Rookery),
Addingham

Fig 15. No. 180, Gilroyd Lane, Linthwaite

Plate 22.
Mill-workers' cottages,
Goose Eye, Laycock

In the textile districts weaving was the most prevalent domestic industrial occupation, but was not the only process conducted in the home. Many of the dwellings which have the outward appearance of typical weavers' cottages would have been occupied by domestic textile workers engaged in other processes such as combing, card-setting and, before mechanization, slubbing.

Cottages were, increasingly, built in close proximity to the mills in which some of the preparatory and finishing processes were carried out. Mechanical power, for centuries only used for the fulling of woollen cloth was, in the course of the 18th century, applied to a number of other processes. Power spinning machinery developed in the 1760s for the cotton industry was modified in the 1780s for use in the worsted trade. In the latter decade power-driven scribbling machinery was also introduced into the woollen industry. Since the new machines were power-driven, they had to be housed in mills which could provide the necessary power. This bringing together of the workforce in one building, or group of buildings, resulted in an increase in the number of mill-hands at the expense of domestic workers (Thornes 1981, 14). Cotton and worsteds, the textiles to which the new spinning machinery was first applied, were produced in the upper Aire and Calder valleys and it was in these areas, therefore, that the impact of the new technology was first felt.

These early mills were generally small, that belonging to Thomas Hinchcliffe of Thurstonland, for example, em-ploying only two men, five boys and one girl as late as 1833. There were exceptions, however, a notable one being Wormald, Fountaine and Gott's woollen factory at Bean Ing, Leeds. Because the majority of late 18th and early 19th-century mills were water-powered it was necessary that they should be situated in locations with adequate water flow. The availability of such sources dictated that many mills were situated in isolated rural locations. Low Mill, Addingham, the first worsted spinning mill in the county, built in 1787, was one such; the cotton mill at Goose Eye, Laycock, established in 1790, was another. The isolated locations of these mills made it necessary for the mill owners to provide accommodation in order to attract workers and ensure a reliable on the spot workforce (Pl 22).[1] In the case of the large woollen factory at Bean Ing, on the western outskirts of Leeds, it was the sheer size of its workforce rather than its location which made the provision of housing necessary.

Typical mill-workers' cottages, as in the case of those built for weavers, were terraced two-storeyed dwellings with no back door and a single room on each floor. This type of house, unlike the weavers' cottage, functioned purely as living accommodation, which resulted in slight differences. There was no need for taking-in doors or inter-communication, and the windows could be made smaller since it was not necessary to provide light to work by. The two-storeyed cottages at Low Mill, Addingham (1), probably built soon after the mill was established in

Plate 23.
Cottages with
workfloor above,
Low Mill, Addingham

Plate 24 (*right*).
Cottages with
workfloor above,
Town Street, Armley

1787, are typical of the sort of cottage provided for mill-workers. Economies were sometimes made on land and materials by providing an additional storey for industrial accommodation above the cottages. These floors were similar to the shared workshops provided above some weavers' cottages (see p 18 above), but, unlike many of these, they were cut off entirely from the living accommodation; nor were they necessarily used for weaving. At Low Mill a lofty workshop (or warehouse) ran over a block of two-storeyed cottages and mill premises (2) (Pl 23) and similarly in Town Street, Armley (5), a third-storey workfloor ran over four two-storeyed cottages (Pl 24). In this case a carriageway leads through to a rear courtyard and above it is a trap-door by means of which materials could be raised to the workfloor from carts below.

The increasing capitalization of the industry meant that those who were investing money in mill ventures were more likely than their predecessors to have, or be able to

Plate 25. Cottages in farm complex, Marsh Lane, Southowram

Plate 26. Cottages and barn, Green End, Old Town

acquire, capital with which to finance workers' housing. Employers of hand-loom weavers also on occasion provided cottages for their workforce. This would seem to have been the case at The Rookery, Addingham (3), where it is likely that the owner of the loomshop also built the sixteen back-to-back cottages associated with it.

Finance for building cottages for both weavers and millhands came from a wide variety of other sources. Some unconnected with the industry built cottages as an invest-ment, intending the rents to provide an income for themselves and their dependents. Farmers, for example, took advantage of the demand for accommodation and built cottages for textile workers, often building them onto farmhouses or converting outbuildings. Some of these cottages may have housed farm labourers, but there would not have been sufficient agricultural work to occupy all the inhabitants of developments such as those along Meltham Road, Marsden (84), or off Marsh Lane, Southowram (119)

Plate 27. Cottages and barn, Wellhouse Fields, Golcar

Plate 28. Crowther Fold, Harden

(Pl 25). The row of six cottages at Green End, Old Town (148), built in 1825 and with a barn at one end, may well have been erected by a farmer and likewise that at Wellhouse Fields, Upper Wellhouse (41) (Pls 26, 27).

Other providers of cottage property were estate owners eager to increase their income from rents, like the Saviles, who encouraged the development of the textile industry on their estate in the Colne Valley. They developed Golcar as a cloth-workers' settlement in the late 18th and early 19th

centuries, followed by Scapegoat Hill in the second quarter of the 19th century. Further north, and on a smaller scale, Benjamin Ferrand built on his estate a row of three cottages at Crowther Fold, Harden (8) in 1776 (Pl 28).

Not all prospective investors owned land which they could develop; some had to buy property before they could build. One such was William Thorpe, a gentleman from London, who in 1826 bought some farmland near Sowerby. On this he built a row of six cottages known as Thorpe

Plate 29. Club Houses, Old Town

Place (123), which was extended by another six houses shortly afterwards (Deeds). The 1841 Census records that all the working inhabitants were weavers and a low, single-storey building in front of the terrace may have provided additional weaving accommodation as a loomshop. It seems that Thorpe always intended the cottages for weavers which would explain why the cottages were larger than many others built at the time, containing two rooms on each floor. Another smaller-scale investor, probably typical of many, was Joseph Beaumont, a shoemaker of Holmfirth. Beaumont built a pair of three-storeyed cottages at Gully *c*.1794 to rent out, probably to weavers to judge by their appearance. The intention was that the rent from the property would provide a guaranteed income for his daughters (Cunnington 1980, 213; Thornes 1981, 20).

There is a fine distinction between those who built houses as an investment and those who built them as a speculative venture. Investors retained ownership of the property, seeing their return in the rents they collected, while speculators sold the houses as soon as they had been built to make an immediate profit. During the boom period of the late 18th century such speculations could be extremely profitable. In 1796 James Graham split some of his farms in the Leeds area into plots of land of 5 to 10 acres. On each of these he built clothiers' houses 'every one of which', he said, 'was immediately taken at almost any price I chose to fix'. The success of Graham's scheme encouraged other land-owners to follow his example (Thornes 1981, 20). The houses they built were of the larger variety for clothiers and wealthier weavers who were practising a dual economy of industry and agriculture. Apart from some ventures in the towns aimed only indirectly at textile workers, there seems to have been little speculative building of the smallest type of cottage at that time. This was probably because smaller cottages would have been easier to lease than sell to textile workers, the majority of whom did not have the means to buy them.

Workers may have been unable to buy cottages directly but, through joining building clubs, were able to do so indirectly. In the course of the 18th century numerous clubs and friendly societies were formed which, in return for a regular subscription fee, offered some sort of financial insurance against ill health, old age, unemployment and other vicissitudes. By the late 18th century several of these friendly societies and clubs had turned their attention to building houses for their members. One such body was the Loyal Georgian Society, founded in Halifax as a mutual benefit society in 1779 during a period of economic difficulty. Early in its history the society lent money to its members to build houses. The success of this venture eventually encouraged the members to found the Halifax Permanent Building Society (Hobson 1953, 17). The members of the Loyal Georgian Society were mainly small businessmen, but there were other clubs which catered for those of more limited means. They, too, subscribed regularly and as soon as the club, or terminating building society, was able to do so it bought a plot of land and began to build houses using the club members' labour and skills in order to save on expenses. As each house was built it was allocated to a member by lottery, or rented out until all the members could be housed. Once this task was completed the club was wound up. Within West Yorkshire the many terraces called Club Row, or Club Houses, bear witness to the building club movement. For the most part they are located in the textile districts, where there was a demand for housing and there were also those with money available to subscribe. The terrace of two and three-storeyed cottages at Old Town (147) known as 'Club Houses' is one such row (Pl 29) and another possible example is a row of three-storeyed houses built in 1820 in Knowle Road, Crimble. Each of the houses in Knowle Road has a datestone with a different set of initials, which implies that the houses were built by, or for, different people and yet as part of a single development.

Men of lesser means built smaller cottages. Numbers 1–7 Strike Lane, Skelmanthorpe (30), were built in 1822 by the Golden Fleece Friendly Society (Wainwright pers. comm.). In size and design these four dwellings are similar to other club-built cottages and are no different to those provided by other types of builder. The Strike Lane cottages each contain a living-room with a chamber above used for weaving and a small barrel-vaulted cellar provided additional food storage space (Fig 16). The cottages in Club Row, Wilsden (155), built in 1832, similarly originally comprised a single living-room with a chamber above (Fig 17).

Textile workers' cottages were situated in a variety of locations, these being generally determined by the role their occupant played in the industry. For example, the dwellings of cottage-workers who were self-employed or had work put-out to them were often clustered together in hamlets. Typically, some earlier habitation or settlement would act as a nucleus for these. New Longley, Norland, and Oldfield, Honley, are examples of hamlets where the earliest dwelling

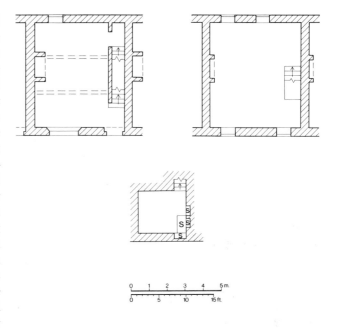

Fig 16. No. 5, Strike Lane, Skelmanthorpe

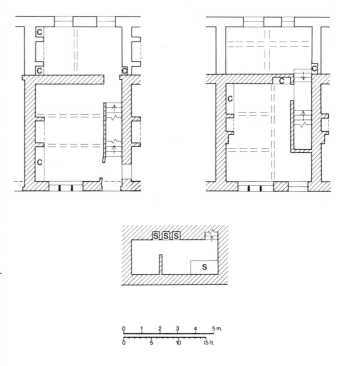

Fig 17. No. 6, Club Row, Wilsden

Plate 30. Weavers' cottages, Little London, Rawdon

was a farm around which grew the settlement. At Hepton-stall an existing village formed a nucleus to which many new textile workers' cottages were added in the early 19th century. In some cases the size of settlements grew rapidly, one example being Little London, Rawdon, a comparatively large village which consists almost entirely of late 18th- and early 19th-century weavers' cottages (Pl 30).

When the cottagers were employed by a master clothier, on his premises or in their own homes, their dwellings were often built near that of the employer. At Ryecroft, for example, cottages were built near to the master clothier's house at about the time that it was heightened by a loomshop storey for the purpose of providing working accommodation for a larger number of weavers. Not all the cottagers living in this development would have worked in the loomshop, however, for in several of the dwellings there was provision for domestic weaving.

Agriculture

In agriculture, as in textiles, workers benefited from the diversion of capital into housing. One conspicuous provider of accommodation for the rural population, particularly in the east of the county, was the large estate owner. Philanthropy provided one of the motivations of estate owners to build cottages for their workers, together with a growing feeling that it was a landlord's responsibility to provide accommodation for those who lived and worked on his estate. Surviving documentary records show how these sentiments were expressed at Harewood when Edwin Lascelles rebuilt the village in the late 18th century. At the time that the work was done, between approximately 1796 and 1812, most of the people living in Harewood worked on Lascelles' estate. One of his philanthropic gestures was to establish a ribbon factory to provide an additional means of employment for its population (Jewell 1819, 12); he also built a school and allowed tenants to rent small plots of land on which to keep a cow or two to supplement their incomes (Survey 1796, 108, 122). The new cottages (43) which Lascelles provided were of a better standard than those they replaced. The old cottages were built of stone with thatched, or occasionally tile, roofs. Some of these were described as hovels, while others were more comparable in size to the new two-storeyed dwellings. The new houses were de-

Plate 31. L-shaped block of estate cottages at Harewood

Plate 32. Estate cottages, Harewood

signed by John Carr, who had recently completed Harewood House for Lascelles, and were built stylishly in the Palladian manner (Pl 31). The rebuilding scheme was conducted with regard to the tenants' convenience and welfare, cottagers being moved into their new homes as they were completed, after which their old dwellings were demolished. An estate survey made in 1796 records this process in action: 'The six following Cottages are taking down and the Tenants removed to new Dwellings, as they are finished ready for their Reception' (Survey 1796, 137).

The two-storeyed dwellings were built of stone with stone roofs. Carr's cottages varied in size, some of them being small enough to be described as 'of rather a meaner kind' (Survey 1796, 136; Pl 32). The majority, however, were more like the 'newly erected Range of Buildings' described as

containing four Dwellings on the same plan as the rest of the Village – vizt – two small Rooms below and one above, with coal house and small yard behind, very complete, recently finished (Survey 1796, 137).

Plate 33. Brick Row, West Bretton

Several of the dwellings were provided with a shop or workplace either in the cottage or the yard, while larger houses were provided for the doctor, the vicar and two school teachers.

The desire to create a favourable impression was much in evidence at Harewood. As well as providing improved accommodation for the tenants, the new housing enhanced the estate. It supplied an impressive backcloth for Lascelles' recently built house and one that reflected creditably on himself. No doubt this consideration influenced Lascelles to some degree, the closing remarks made about the Harewood cottages in the 1796 Survey reflecting his motives:

> These Comfortable Habitations reflect great Honour and Praise on their Noble Owner, who at this time is extending his Praiseworthy munificence, by an increase of these necessary, but in general, too much neglected Buildings – The Example is highly meritous and consonant to the Grandeur of the Place it adjoins; and it is to be lamented that Gentlemen of Landed Property do not attend more to such laudable and Charitable Acts (Survey 1796, 146).

Such praise would have been welcomed by Lascelles, who himself felt the village to be worthy of a tour of inspection by the Grand Duke Nicholas of Russia in 1816 (Buckle 1975, 23).

At much the same time as Lascelles was rebuilding Harewood, a row of seven cottages was erected on the Bretton Hall estate. These, too, were built to a higher standard than was usual in labourers' cottages. They are distinguished in appearance, with three bay windows in a front elevation unbroken by doors (Pl 33). Inside, entry was into a passage rather than directly into the living-room and on the first floor, as in the Harewood cottages, there were two bedrooms rather than the usual single chamber (Fig 18). The appearance of the West Bretton cottages is further distinguished by their being built of brick, the same material as was used for some of the cottages on the Nostell estate at Foulby and for others in Barwick-in-Elmet. In contrast to their stone-built neighbours, these cottages would have stood out and may well have been built with that purpose in mind. Further west in the county, a range of cottages on the Lister-Kaye estate at Denby Grange was built of stone to a

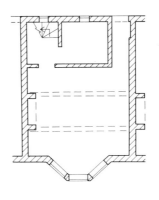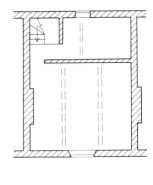

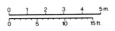

Fig 18. No.4, Brick Row, West Bretton

Plate 34. Sandygate farmhouse, Paris, Holmfirth

simple back-to-back plan, but the cottages were disting-uished, nonetheless, by their position as part of a formal courtyard and by the small attic windows which took the form of oculi in the gables. Again it would seem that appearance was of some importance to the builder.

Estate housing is found for the most part in the east of the county in which area estates were an important employer of rural labour. In the upland, western part of the county the land was more frequently divided into smaller holdings. In both areas agricultural labourers would have lived in cottages indistinguishable from those occupied by other workers, but in the later 18th and early 19th century a new type of dwelling began to be built in the upland areas reflecting developments in farming practice. During this period, large areas of marginal and common land were enclosed (WYAS, H.Q. English 1965). The reclaimed land was frequently divided into relatively small plots, resulting in the creation of many new farms of modest size (RCHM forthcoming, ch 6). On these, farmhouses were erected either by the farmers themselves or by estate owners for tenants, as when Christopher Rawson enclosed an area of

moorland in Erringdon (c.1836) and divided it into four tenant farms (Stell 1960, 109). The type of farmhouse which Rawson and many others used was the distinctive laithe house plan, in which the house was under the same roof as the barn and cattle stalls. The plan was compact, convenient and economic to build, providing living quarters for the farmer and his family and accommodation for his corn and cattle.

Although the occupants of these houses, unlike most industrial workers, were not wage-earners, in many cases their houses are indistinguishable from those of the latter in terms of accommodation provided. Generally the smallest laithe houses had a living-room and scullery or two living-rooms on the ground floor, and two bedrooms above (see Pl 34). In the first half of the 19th century, however, the wealth and status of the occupants appears to have declined, the size of many of the smallest Pennine laithe houses being reduced to a living-room and scullery on the ground floor with a single bedroom above (RCHM forthcoming, ch 6; Stell 1960, 121). In this form the laithe house offered no more accommodation than many contemporary cottages.

28

THE EXTRACTIVE INDUSTRIES

The three most important extractive industries in West Yorkshire in the late eighteenth century were stone quarrying, the working of iron ore and coal mining. Although there was quarrying activity throughout the country, it was particularly important in the central and western areas, where the many outcrops of Sandstone and Millstone Grit provided building stone of good quality. By the early 18th century the iron industry was concentrated in the south of the county, in which area the Tankersley ironstone was easily accessible (Thornes 1981, 28–30). This industry has left many marks upon the landscape, but few recognizable structures associated with it survive. Coal mining in the same period was, like quarrying, concentrated in the central and western areas of the county. These three industries were, for the most part, confined to meeting limited local demands and, therefore, operated on a small scale, each working employing only a few workmen (Goodchild 1978, 7 and Holmes 1967, 40). A colliery in Hunslet, for example, when advertised for sale in 1742 provided work for only 15

to 18 men (Goodchild 1978, 9). Moor Pit, in Scholes, employed an average of only sixteen men between 1801 and 1813 (Wilding 1977, 22).

The large numbers of single-storey cottages surviving in the areas where these industries were located strongly indicates that this was the principal type of accommodation occupied by quarry and mine workers. Documentary evidence confirms that it is in cottages like these that many miners lived. In the Bowling area it was said that 'the opening up of the coal measures [at the beginning of the 19th century] . . . brought into existence a number of low one-storey houses . . . which somehow were considered good enough for colliers' (Cudworth 1891, 325). A parliamentary enquiry conducted some years later reveals that miners' cottages in Flockton were equally small, also that they were overcrowded, sparsely furnished and poorly maintained (Parliamentary Papers 1842, 217–19).

It is only from the late 18th century onwards, however, that identifiable examples of this type of house survive in any numbers, particularly dense concentrations occurring to the south and south west of Bradford and to the east of

Plate 35. Single-storey cottage, Burnt Side Road, New Farnley

Huddersfield. There are numerous examples at Grange Moor, Shelf Moor, and around Upper Moorside, New Farnley (Pl 35), all of which were areas of extensive mining and quarrying activity.

The relative impermanence and small scale of individual workings in the extractive industries to some extent determined the sources of capital made available for building houses for the workers in those industries. This impermanence discouraged most categories of potential investors from building houses for these classes of workmen. The dwellings that were built, therefore, tended to be of simple design and construction which were cheap to build. The single-storey cottage was the type which best fulfilled these criteria.

Towards the end of the 18th century these extractive industries expanded considerably and, as in the textile industry, their increasingly capitally intensive nature affected the type of accommodation provided for the workforces. Increasing demand for both domestic and industrial buildings in the late 18th and early 19th century had a significant effect on the quarrying industry – the growing market for stone being met by the development of larger and relatively permanent concerns.

Single-storey cottages continued to be built in some quarrying districts, for example in the area around Mountain, Queensbury. Other quarry workers lived in villages near to their places of work in two-storey cottages. At the same time, small numbers of cottages do seem to have been built by employers for their workforce. Situated next to Thornton Quarry are numbers 65 and 67 Back Heights Road, Moscow (133). It is likely that these were built by or for a quarry owner, and certainly later in the century they belonged to the proprietor of the works. There were also cottages associated with the nearby, isolated Egypt Quarry, which were probably owner-built. In both these cases the cottages followed basic contemporary plans. Numbers 65 and 67 Back Heights Road were two-storeyed blind-back cottages, each containing a ground-floor living-room and first-floor chamber, with entry direct into the living-room (see Fig 19). The cottages at Egypt consisted originally of a block of four back-to-backs to which another two pairs were added separately later in the century (135). The poorer quality, thin stone of which these dwellings were built was probably waste from the quarry. Accommodation provided in each cottage was similar to that in 65 and 67 Back Heights Road, although nos 18 and 20 at Egypt were supplied with wash cellars, these being shared to judge by their external doors.

The coal and iron industries also underwent a period of rapid expansion in the late 18th and early 19th centuries. The coal industry was stimulated by a growing demand for fuel for both domestic and industrial purposes, while improve-

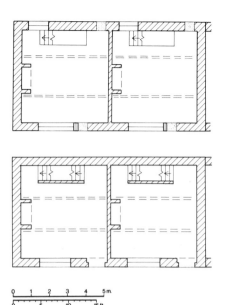

Fig 19. Nos. 65 and 67, Back Heights Road, Moscow

ments in the transport system opened up wider markets to mines in a number of parts of the coalfield (Thornes 1981, 36, 46–9). Technological developments made possible the more efficient exploitation of the coalfield, increasing the competitiveness of those collieries which could afford to invest in pumps, winding engines and rail and waggonway systems. The importance of acquiring such equipment meant that increasingly large sums of money were needed to finance mining, and as the scale of the industry grew it was increasingly difficult for smaller collieries to compete with the larger concerns (Lewis 1971, 41).

Technological developments had an equally significant effect on the iron industry. The change from charcoal to coke for fuel for blast furnaces and from water to steam-power for the blowing of those furnaces influenced the future location of ironworks. As a result, the establishment of the new generation of ironworks required larger capital investment than had been the case previously.

In West Yorkshire the majority of these ironworks were situated in the ironstone and coal-rich area to the south of Bradford. They were no longer simply furnaces, but integrated manufacturing complexes mining their own raw materials and producing a wide variety of finished articles, ranging from steam-engines and bridges to armaments and iron railings.

The increasing size of many mining and ironworking concerns resulted in the recruitment of substantially larger workforces. At Middleton Colliery, for example, the number of employees rose from about seventy-seven in

Plate 36 (*left*).
Nos. 9 and 11,
Green End Road, Wibsey

Plate 37 (*below*).
Colliers' Row, Wrose

Plate 38. Nos. 37 and 38, Hird Road, Low Moor

1773 to 320 by 1820 (Rimmer 1955, 41) this increased workforce requiring accommodation. In those areas where the single-storey cottage was a traditional form, this type of dwelling continued to be built. Numbers 39–51 Green End Road, Wibsey, for example, are a row of seven one-roomed cottages built in the early 19th century (Pl 36). There are numerous other examples of single-storey cottages in the area, both of the one- and two-roomed variety, with and without scullery outshuts. Many of these dwellings would have been occupied by coal and ironstone miners (Dodsworth 1971, 133), although colliers and ironworkers also lived in two-storeyed cottages similar to those occupied by other workers. The parliamentary report on Flockton colliers reveals that some of them lived in two-storeyed cottages which were comparable to those which survive in Colliers' Row, Wrose (64) (Pl 37). This terrace was built in the early 19th century and consisted of four blind-back cottages, each containing a living-room with bedroom above. A similar sort of cottage was provided for some workers near to the Low Moor Ironworks. 38 Hird Road (97) (Pl 38, Fig 20) is one in a row of three typical one-up/one-down, blind-back cottages, superior in quality to the many single-storey cottages in the area.

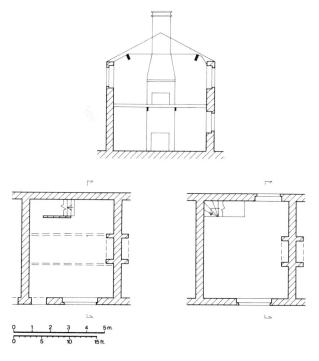

Fig 20. No. 38, Hird Road, Low Moor

Plate 39. Short Row, Low Moor

It is not clear who built these cottages, but it is probable that many were erected by the occupants themselves. Others, however, were provided by colliery and ironworks' owners. When John Elwell and John Crawshaw leased the mineral rights at Shelf in 1793, they received permission to build not only the necessary furnaces, but also 'habitations for workers' on the common land of the Manor (Norman 1969, 77). At Middleton the miners' contracts included accommodation, in order to provide which the colliery had to build new cottages in the 1790s and first years of the 19th century (Rimmer 1955, 43). Shortly before this the Fentons had established a colliery village at Belle Isle, Middleton, and in the early 19th century provided three-roomed cottages at Waterloo near their Rothwell colliery (Goodchild 1978, 70). Unfortunately, little physical evidence remains of these early colliery housing schemes. An exception to this is the Low Moor area of Bradford. The records of the Low Moor Iron Company show that from 1795 it was spending money on renting houses. In 1801 the Company embarked on a policy of cottage building, spending £700 in that year on 'thirteen new houses built in Wibsey' (WYAS Bradford, Low Moor Stock Book 1795–1835). Such expenditure, however, could only be undertaken by large companies with a ready supply of capital.

The Low Moor Iron Company, in common with other large employers of labour, would have had a number of

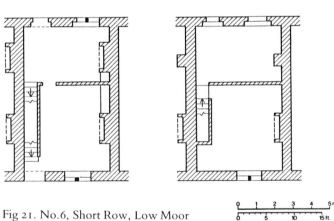

Fig 21. No.6, Short Row, Low Moor

motives for supplying housing. In some cases there was an element of altruism and concern for the workers' well-being. William Fenton included a school in his housing development at Waterloo (Goodchild 1978, 70) and the Low Moor Iron Company was similarly concerned to provide some sort of education for its workers' children (Dodsworth 1971, 133–4, 149). No doubt employers were influenced also by the fact that employees living near the works were more punctual and reliable than those who lived at a distance. The former also could be controlled by the threat of eviction. Perhaps the greatest incentive for house building, however, was the need to attract workers in the first instance.

The rapid growth of the collieries and ironworks at the turn of the century meant that they were competing for labour. The strength of the miners' position was shown by the success of the Middleton colliers in obtaining wage increases in 1786, 1791 and 1801 (Rimmer 1955, 45) and by the difficulties encountered by the Bowling Hall Estate steward, who in 1799 wrote that he had 'had some trouble with the colliers wanting more wages' (Cudworth 1891, 209). Employers needed to do all they could to attract workers who possessed skills which were in demand, a problem which was particularly acute in the iron industry. At Low Moor amongst the first cottages to be erected by the Company were Furnace and Forge Rows, the latter of which survives, although now known as Short Row (101, Pl 39, Fig 21). It seems that Short Row was built in order to attract such skilled workers, for the six cottages were superior in quality and design to other housing in the area. Each cottage had a back as well as a front door and contained two large ground-floor rooms, both of which were heated, two bedrooms and a cellar. In addition, they were provided with a small front garden and an allotment at the rear. In 1841 this terrace was occupied by forgemen, moulders, smiths, model-makers and a manager, all skilled foundry workers whose expertise was reflected in the higher standard of accommodation with which the Company provided them.

Transport

The growth of the county's transport network, in particular the canal and turnpike road systems, greatly facilitated the development of the economy of the area as a whole. In 1699 Royal Assent was granted to an act to allow the rivers Aire and Calder to be made navigable downstream of Leeds and Wakefield, respectively. The major period of canal construction began with the building of the Calder and Hebble navigation, for which Royal Assent was granted in 1758. This was followed by the opening of a number of canals which, by 1825, connected many West Yorkshire towns with the national navigable waterways system (Priestley 1831). Concurrent with this canal building activity, the county's road system was improved by the construction of turnpikes, these being built particularly in the years 1750–9 and 1820–9 (Goodchild 1961).

From documentary sources it is apparent that from an early date the canal companies and turnpike trusts provided accommodation for some categories of employees, principally lock-keepers and toll-collectors. In 1753 riots directed against the toll system resulted in the destruction of toll-bars and their associated cottages, some of these dwellings being burnt down on more than one occasion (Cudworth 1891, 197). Early lock-keepers' cottages may have existed on the Aire and Calder Navigation, for the Commissioners' Plan of 1775 shows some dwellings situated at the locks. The earliest cottages which survive, however, date to the end of the 18th century.

Canal construction provided employment for a large workforce but only rarely was accommodation provided by the canal companies for their navvies. One exception was at Standedge, above Marsden. Here a tunnel was cut through the Pennines between 1794 and 1811 as part of the construction of the canal through the Pennines from Huddersfield to Ashton-under-Lyme, in Cheshire (Schofield 1981, 19). In this instance the scale of the project made it necessary for the canal company to build a number of cottages to house their workers; of these houses all that now remains are the shells of three one-up/one-down cottages next to the engine-house at Redbrooke (88) and a single cottage at Gilberts (86). The latter originally formed part of a row of six two-storeyed cottages built adjoining an earlier laithe house. Although these cottages were relatively spacious, each containing two rooms on each floor, it is probable that a number of lodgers would also have been housed in them, as was the custom for housing labourers involved in the construction of reservoirs later in the 19th century.

Accommodation was more commonly provided for other categories of canal workers. Where the Huddersfield Narrow Canal emerged from the Pennines above Marsden, a pair of cottages were erected for the tunnel keepers (89) (Pl 40). These were large cottages, each containing two rooms

Plate 40. Tunnel End Cottages, Standedge

Plate 41. Keeper's cottage, Ramsden's Bridge, Stanley Ferry

and a scullery on the ground floor, with two bedrooms above. A stable adjoining them is likely to have sheltered company horses. Similar provision was made at the Stanley swing-bridge operator's cottage on the Aire and Calder Navigation (Pl 41, Fig 22). This single-storey dwelling (130) contained three rooms, beneath which ran two cellars (Fig 22). One of these had external access only and is said to have been used as a stable for the company's horses.

The Calder and Hebble Navigation Company's canal works department provided accommodation for employees at a number of points along its route, the main phase of building activity occurring between 1770 and 1834. On the quay at Elland, a three-roomed single-storey cottage was built c.1820 for the wharfinger (35) (Pl 42). At much the same time a larger house was constructed at the Salterhebble junction with the Halifax branch of the canal (118) (Pl 43).

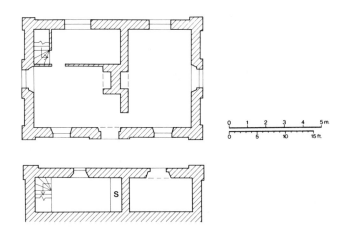

Fig 22. Keeper's Cottage, Ramsden's Bridge, Stanley Ferry

Plate 42. Wharfinger's cottage, Elland Quay

Plate 43. Lock-keeper's cottage, Salterhebble

Plate 44. Lock-keeper's cottage, Brookfoot

The occupant of this dwelling not only minded the lock, but also supervised two nearby canal basins. Smaller cottages were provided at other locks. That at Brookfoot (108) (Pl 44; Fig 23) was built in 1808, to the same plan as the one at Elland Lock (Pl 45). In both cottages the central portion of the façade projected, thereby giving a good view of traffic approaching along the canal from either direction. Although this seems to have been a useful functional feature, the Navigation Company had only one other lock cottage built to this design, the rest being constructed without the projecting bay and in a variety of shapes and sizes (Plan Book 1834, passim).

The design of the toll-collectors' cottages built at intervals along the turnpike roads was influenced by requirements similar to those of lock-keepers. In both cases it was desirable that the occupant should have a good view from his cottage of approaching traffic. At Wragby the result of these corresponding needs was the construction of a cottage (53) whose plan was almost identical to those of the

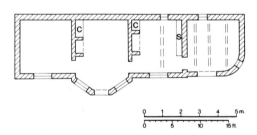

Fig 23. Lock-keeper's cottage, Brookfoot

dwellings at Brookfoot and Elland locks (Pl 46). It, too, has a projecting bay giving a good view of traffic, in this case along the Redhouse and Crofton Turnpike Road. Other turnpike cottages were influenced by the same functional consideration. The hexagonal cottage at Steanor Bottom (140) was positioned so that, as well as the main turnpike road, an approach road could be observed (Pl 47). The same idea is illustrated by the design of a cottage at Heckmond-

Plate 45. Keeper's cottage, Elland Lock

Plate 46. Bar House, Wragby

Plate 47. Toll House, Steanor Bottom

Plate 48. Toll House, No.134, Huddersfield Road, Heckmondwike

wike (47), the projecting, hexagonally shaped porch of which gave a view of traffic approaching along two roads and in both directions (Pl 48). From surviving cottages and sketches of others (WYAS, Wakefield RT41: Huddersfield and New Hey Turnpike Road), it would seem that even if no portion of the cottage projected to command a view of the road, the whole dwelling was placed jutting out into it to give the same effect. The vulnerability of such cottages to subsequent road schemes probably accounts for the lack of surviving examples.

The canal and turnpike cottages were provided by the respective companies and trusts primarily for reasons of necessity. This motive certainly appears to have underlain the provision of labourers' accommodation at Redbrook (88) and Gilberts (86) above Standedge tunnel, where the worksites were particularly remote and inhospitable. It is clear, from a progress report made to the Company shareholders in 1796, that the cottage and workshops were built 'on the mountain' in order to benefit the Company by preventing 'repetition of those delays and loss of time which have been already experienced in sinking the deep pits' (Schofield 1983, 25). In their eye-catching positions alongside the canals and roads the turnpike and lock-keepers' cottages were an aspect of companies' and trusts' public face. That they were seen as such is evident from the fact that many of these cottages were given architectural embellishments seldom found in other workers' houses. The cottage at Stanley swing-bridge, for example, was designed in a classical style (Pl 41). Similarly, the turnpike cottages at Steanor Bottom (140); Heckmondwike (47) and Wragby (53) are all well-built and apparently architect-designed (see Pls 45–7 above).

The cottage at Steanor Bottom is unusual amongst turnpike cottages in being two-storeyed. Despite this it offered no more accommodation than the single-storeyed ones, which generally contained two heated rooms with sometimes an additional pantry or even, in the case of

Plate 49.
Bar Cottage, Rowley Lane, Lepton

Wragby, a third room. Specifications for such a cottage survive in a contract made by the Wakefield to Halifax Turnpike Trust for the construction of a toll cottage at Lightcliffe, Bailiff Bridge in 1805. The building was reminiscent of an earlier toll cottage at Lepton of c.1780 (73) (Pl 49, Fig 24). The contract for the Lightcliffe cottage records that Daniel Naylor, a local mason, was to

> erect, build and completely finish a Turnpike House of two Rooms on a Ground floor of the following dimensions within, to wit, the north room fifteen feet square and the south room fifteen feet by twelve . . . with a pantry six feet by nine and a convenient necessary house (WYAS, Wakefield RT 94).

Because these cottages could be envisaged as symbols of prestige and because once built they would be required to provide many years service, the companies constructed them soundly. That this was the case is evident from the surviving examples; it is also illustrated by the contract for the Lightcliffe cottage in which the turnpike trustees declared that it should be built 'well and substantially' and 'in a workmanlike manner'. Although such cottages offered no more accommodation than other workers' dwellings, there may be some truth in a contemporary ditty

> Contented in my little house,
> On every call I wait,
> To take the toll, to ope and shut
> The five-barr'd turnpike gate

> (Clegg 1915, 334).

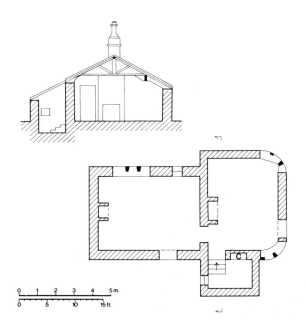

Fig 24. Bar Cottage, Rowley Lane, Lepton

URBAN HOUSING

The expansion of West Yorkshire's economy in the late 18th and early 19th centuries resulted in a phenomenal growth in population, much of which was concentrated in the towns and villages of the manufacturing districts (see Table). Industrial development of the townships of Holbeck and Hunslet, for example, was so rapid in this period that, by 1806, contemporaries considered them to be industrial suburbs of Leeds (Rimmer 1963, 173).

Town	Population in 1801	Population in 1821	Increase (per cent)
Bradford	6,393	13,064	104.35
Halifax	8,886	12,628	42.11
Huddersfield	7,268	13,284	82.77
Leeds	30,669	48,603	61.73
Wakefield	8,131	10,764	32.38

(Chalklin 1974, 39)

This trend was a consequence partly of natural increase, but more significantly of the immigration of workers from the surrounding countryside. In the township of Horbury, it was complained that

> we have between four hundred and five hundred houses and there are eighty houses standing empty; the hands have removed to Leeds and Huddersfield to the merchant manufacturers

> (Glover 1959, 75)

Other immigrants came from further afield: Irish workers, for example, flocked to the county's principal towns in the first half of the 19th century. From wherever it originated, however, this increased urban population needed accommodation of some sort, resulting in an intensification of demand for housing. In Leeds it has been estimated that between 1774 and 1839 the number of houses increased sevenfold.

In those urban areas where the number of inhabitants had continued to increase throughout the 18th century, land available for building within the town boundaries had already been fully developed. The continuing demand for building land on the outskirts of these areas now encouraged land owners to sell their estates in part or whole. In this way undeveloped land came onto the market and building beyond original town boundaries became an increasingly common feature of urban development. One example of such development was the Wilson family's Leeds estate, which was gradually broken-up, sold, and covered with housing and commercial premises. East of the town centre, workers' housing began to cover the Marsh Lane area (Beresford 1974, 288).

Fig 25. Paley's developments, East Leeds (Beresford, 1974)

Urban housing developments designed for the accommodation of workmen were generally speculative ventures. Some employers provided housing for their workers, but usually only those with large labour requirements since, in most cases, there was a sufficiently large pool of labour available within the towns to make it unnecessary for employers to try and attract it by providing accommodation. Instead, the provision of housing was left to others who were more than willing to take on the task in return for the concomitant financial gain. One contemporary observed in 1842 that

> In periods of prosperity, no property is more valuable than what is called cottage property in towns; for the demand for labour enables the operatives to pay a high rent, which, for the most part, is collected weekly or quarterly, according to the character of the tenantry. Thus whole streets of houses have arisen in Leeds, in an inconceivably short space of time, and in many instances evidently for the sole end of speculation, without regard to the absolute want of the tenants (Baker 1842, 358).

One of those who built 'for the sole end of speculation' in Leeds was Richard Kendall, a pocket-book maker, who, by the early 19th century had developed a block of sixty-five cottages in the East Ward. Another, operating on an even larger scale, was the entrepreneur Richard Paley. From 1787

Plate 50.
Wormald Yard,
Huddersfield

Plate 51. Turks Head Yard, Briggate, Leeds

Plate 52. Hollidays Court, Leeds

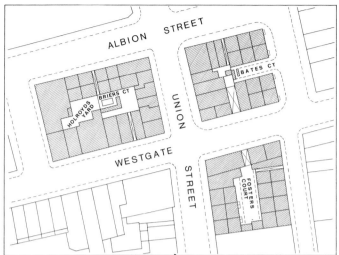

Fig 26. Court developments, Halifax

Paley bought and sold land for housing development, building on some of it himself and selling the remainder. By 1803 he had built about 275 houses, most of them in the eastern area of the town, while 290 more had been built on land sold by him to other speculators (Beresford 1974, 292, 297–8; Fig 25). He also sold land to building clubs, a number of which were established in Leeds by the 1780s.

Although the membership of these clubs comprised the more affluent tradesmen and artisans, these members did not always subscribe in order to house themselves, but, rather, to build properties which they then rented out to workers with lower incomes. Much of the Marsh Lane and Quarry Hill area of Leeds was developed by such clubs (Beresford 1974, 303) and in Halifax they built on the relatively cheap building land by Hebble Brook (Hobson 1953, 151).

Both the building clubs and the speculative developers built houses which, for the most part, were similar to those provided for workers elsewhere in the county. The two or three-storeyed blind-back cottage with a single room on each floor had already established itself as a common urban type, being a form well-suited to the building up of narrow yards. In Huddersfield Wormald Yard (63) (Pl 50) was developed in this manner; the same was also true of yards in other towns, including Leeds (see Pl 51) and Halifax (Fig 26). Although the surviving yard dwellings give some idea of early 19th-century conditions, it must be remembered that those buildings which have survived to the present day were of a sufficiently high standard to escape later slum-clearance, changes in function or modern redevelopment and therefore are not necessarily representative of the poorest workers' accommodation. Hollidays Court, for example, which survives in Leeds (67) (Pl 52), is narrow,

dark and gloomy, but in 1841 it housed relatively affluent workers, including a policeman, a family of whitesmiths and an engineer. The same was true of St John's Court, Leeds (70) (Pl 53, Fig 27), in which lived a butcher and a brewer. One of the cottages even had the dubious advantage of an extra bedroom built above the four privies at the end of the block, a feature which was to be much criticized later in the century.

When previously undeveloped land was built upon, one of the most popular house-plans adopted by the builders was the back-to-back. This type was particularly favoured in Leeds. An early example were those built in Union Street by a building club formed in 1787 (Beresford 1971, 101, 102). Other clubs followed suit and Richard Paley also used this plan extensively in his speculative ventures (Fig 25). The popularity of this cottage type with builders stems from the fact that the first priority of most speculators was to develop property with an eye to the best possible return on initial capital outlay. It must have been evident that by adopting the back-to-back they could achieve greater densities of housing. With their shared back walls and roofs this house-type also economized on building materials, so reducing the cost of each individual dwelling. When there was room to build a terrace only one house deep, this sometimes resulted in the half-back, or 'salt pie', house built as a back-to-back but without the rear dwelling and, therefore, with only a single-pitch roof. By 1801, back-to-backs already comprised nearly 10 per cent of the houses in the borough of Leeds and the proportion continued to rise rapidly (Beresford 1971, 47). The back-to-back dwelling of this period generally comprised a cellar, a living-room and a

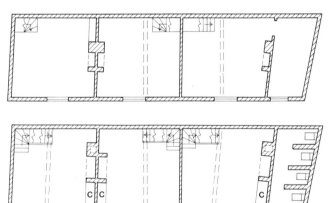

Fig 27. Nos. 2, 3 and 4, St. John's Court, Leeds

chamber; the rooms being 5 yards (4.6m) square with ceilings about 4 yards (3.7m) high (Baker 1842, 359). Writing in 1821, William Brown concluded that housing of this type was superior in quality to the accommodation provided for Scottish workers. He observed that workers in the Leeds flax mills

> are certainly more comfortably lodged, their houses are but two storeys high and each family occupies a whole house, cooking and eating in the lower flat or room and sleeping in the upper. They seem comfortably clean and few are without neat and substantial furniture (Brown 1821, 3).

Plate 54.
Tenement dwellings in
East Leeds

By the late 1830s a back-to-back of this type fetched a rent of between £4 and £7 per annum, which represented between 17 and 20 per cent of the income of those labourers and artisans who lived in them (Baker 1842, 360). Houses built any larger or more spaciously would have been beyond the means of such workers, many of whom could not afford even the smaller back-to-backs. Instead they occupied cheaper, less commodious dwellings offered by novel forms of accommodation which were generally restricted to the urban areas.

One alternative to back-to-backs were the cellar dwellings which existed in all West Yorkshire towns in this period. They comprised 3 per cent of the dwellings in Leeds township in 1842 (Rimmer 1963, 179), there were some 300 in Halifax in 1851 (Bretton 1948, 76) and they were common in Bradford. Generally cellar dwellings comprised only a single room built beneath a cottage, its floor level below that of the street and having a separate entrance, usually reached by steps at the front of the house. These cellars were not necessarily inadequate, often being preferred by tenants to accommodation in subdivided houses or tenements.

Plate 55. Galleried dwellings in East Leeds

Tenement dwellings are referred to in a number of contemporary documents, being 'not at all uncommon in Bradford' (Baker 1842, 356) and known to have been built by Richard Paley in Leeds (Beresford 1974, 307). Tenement dwellings were formed by the horizontal division of a house or block. The lower tenement in these developments was on a level with the street, as in the case of the dwelling-and-underdwelling cottages of the upland areas. Above were tenements which were either two-storeyed with a living-room and a chamber, or comprised only a single room (Baker 1842, 356). These dwellings were reached by one or two tiers of galleries (Pls 54, 55).

Cellar dwellings and tenements were occupied by the poorest town-dwellers such as widows, aged poor and Irish immigrants (Baker 1842, 366), often in overcrowded conditions (Bretton 1948, 76). It was not uncommon for more than one family to share a single dwelling, it being observed in Leeds in 1795 'that amongst the lowest rank of people there is often more than one family to a house' (Wilson 1971, 197). Boot and Shoe Yard in particular was seriously overcrowded: in 1839 there were thirty-four houses in the yard, providing a total of fifty-seven rooms in which lived 340 people (Baker 1833, 2).

The poverty of tenants coupled with the profit margins required by builders often determined the quality of housing provided. Speculators and clubs building for immediate gain tended to build shoddily with poor-quality materials. Much of the housing erected in the East Ward of Leeds in the late 18th century was of this nature. George and Ebenezer Streets, for example, which were developed by building clubs, were already among the most squalid places in Leeds by 1809 (Beresford 1971, 110). A similar situation prevailed in Halifax, where it was said of the workers' housing in 1845 that 'most of the folds [of houses] are very damp and filthy: the seats of poverty and disease' and they were built shoddily because

> the small tradesman, penurious in his habits, will not expend a sixpence for the comfort of his tenant beyond necessity; and the building clubs being composed of many, all having a personal interest in the gains, but none in the comfort of their tenants, will not allow of any expenditure beyond what will secure tenants for the property (Hobson 1953, 151–2).

Poorly-built as these houses may have been, they were not, in themselves, necessarily of a lower standard than those found outside the towns or in other areas of the county. A major problem was the lack of overall control of developments, particularly with regard to housing density, access and the provision of sanitary arrangements. The absence of such controls had more serious implications in urban areas than in the comparatively thinly populated rural ones. William Brown felt that it was not in the houses but in their external provisions that Leeds was deficient: 'The streets, roads and lanes are . . . as irregular, narrow, wet and dirty as any in Scotland' (Brown 1821, 3). In Halifax, likewise, it was deplored that in the areas of cheapest housing

> the drainage, ventilation and cleansing are left to chance, as the public authorities take no notice of such locations (Hobson 1953, 152).

Speculators were more concerned with the construction of housing, which brought them an immediate return, than with providing sanitary and other facilities which did not. The way in which land was developed also hampered the provision of such amenities since land, particularly in Leeds,

was held and sold off in small parcels and consequently developed piecemeal rather than as part of a planned whole. In the central area of Leeds the result was a jumble of yards and courts, overcrowded, poorly ventilated and badly lit. These could not be reached by streets, for to do so would have meant cutting through existing houses, a problem which added to the difficulties of providing sewers and a water supply (Baker 1833, 3, Beresford 1974, 108). Light and free air-flow were restricted by the narrowness of the older yards and, once cottages had been built along one or both sides, there was very little open space left. The yard in front of the houses in Turks Head Yard, Leeds (72) is only 3.05m (10ft) at its widest point, and in Ship Yard (71) 3.45m (11ft 3ins). Even yards such as Wormald Yard in Huddersfield (63), which today appear comparatively wide and spacious, would have been cramped in the early 19th century when the surrounding yards were built-up as well and when the houses, including their cellar-dwellings, were in full occupation. The first Ordnance Survey maps show some examples of this type of high density building. Fosters Court in Halifax (see Fig 26) was one of several crowded developments in that area of the town. The situation did not improve when cheaper land, away from the city centre, was developed. Building plots were still sold off in small parcels. To develop these as densely as possible, back-to-backs were built around a central court which, in turn, might contain yet more dwellings. In Leeds the housing density of one of Richard Paley's developments at Camp Fields (Fig 61) was 100 houses to the acre, while another, in an area between York and Off Streets, contained over 138, even the passages which led to the back houses having rooms built over them (Fig 25). In such a situation light and ventilation were restricted by surrounding buildings, while privy provision and arrangements for the removal of filth and excrement were inadequate if they existed at all. Water supplies, too, were wholly lacking or extremely limited and street paving and cleaning unheard of. It is hardly surprising that in such areas disease and ill-health were endemic, a fact which, more than anything else, drew the attention of sanitary and housing reformers to the living conditions of town-dwellers later in the century.

Notes to Chapter 2
[1] Housing of this sort was built at Goose Eye Mill near Keighley (66); on Coal Hill Lane, Bramley (15); in Dearneside Road, Denby Dale (32), facing into the mill yard and adjoining the mill owner's house; and at Wainstalls, Warley (151), built by the Murgatroyds.
[2] This density compares unfavourably with that at which the majority of working people in England lived by the early 20th century – at thirty to fifty houses to an acre (Rowntree and Pigou 1914, 4). The model village of Saltaire, built at much the same time, had a density of approximately forty houses to the acre (Tarn 1973, 32).

CHAPTER 3

THE DEVELOPMENT OF HOUSE TYPES, BUILDING METHODS AND STANDARDS

From the late 18th century capital originating from a wide variety of sources was utilized on an unprecedented scale for the provision of housing for the working population of West Yorkshire. Within half a century this trend was to transform the county's housing stock. In this period the single-storey cottage, the traditional workman's dwelling, began to be replaced by a new form, typically a two-storey house built in a terrace. During the late 18th and early 19th centuries such terraces became progressively longer, a reflection of the rapidly growing and densely concentrated population of the county's manufacturing districts. By this period units of production were tending to grow in size, so concentrating increasingly large numbers of workers in particular areas. This, in turn, encouraged investment in

larger-scale housing developments in those areas. Representative of this phase are two long terraces in Burley-in-Wharfedale (16, 17; Pl 56, Fig 28) each consisting of twelve cottages, and the crescent of twenty-four dwellings on

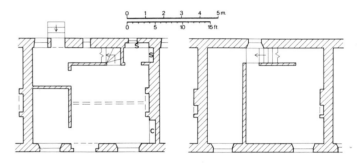

Fig 28 (*above*).
No. 90, Main Street,
Burley in Wharfedale

Plate 56.
Nos. 86–108, Main Street,
Burley in Wharfedale

Plate 57. Nos. 51–92, Bradford Road, Otley

Bradford Road, Otley (104) built in the second quarter of the 19th century (Pl 57, Fig 29). Longer rows were not necessarily the result of one building phase. Often rows of two, three or four cottages were added to at a later date when the builder could afford to do so. Club Row, Wilsden (155), for example, now stands as a terrace of ten houses, but was built up in three phases (Pl 58). Similarly, the block of four back-to-backs at Egypt (135) provided an original core to which a further two pairs were later added. The stages in the development of individual, phase-built, terraces are often evident from the straight joints between houses and in slight differences in the style of gutter brackets, windows and other elements. Other terraces, however, may have been built in phases although no obvious indication of this has been left. Some long terraces may have been developed like Silver Street, Heptonstall (50), where the original intention to further extend the row southwards is indicated by the fact that the stones in the front and back walls at one end have been left projecting (Pl 59). If the row had been continued and the terrace finished off there would have been no sign of this piecemeal evolution.

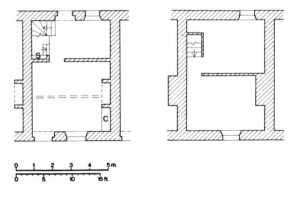

Fig 29. No. 71, Bradford Road, Otley

Cottages built in this period share certain characteristic plan elements. The basic accommodation provided both in single-storey and two-storey cottages consisted of a living-room and second room with perhaps a pantry or cellar for food storage. The living-room was also used for preparing food, eating, working, and might also be used for sleeping. The simplest dwellings, such as the underdwellings of 7–12

Plate 58 (*above*).
Club Row, Wilsden

Plate 59 (*left*).
Silver Street, Heptonstall

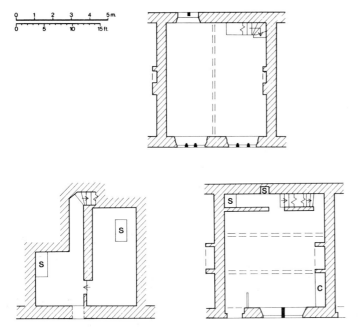

Fig 30. No.26, Upper Reins, Honley

West Laithe, Heptonstall (52) (Fig 12), might contain only this one room. By the early 19th century, however, there was generally a second room which served as the sleeping chamber. In the case of weavers and others who worked in their homes, this latter room might also serve as a workroom. In weavers' cottages in the Bradford area of c.1830 it was said that

> a pair of handlooms and a bobbin wheel would be found in company with a delf case and an oaken chest or 'ark' containing malt or meal. If the delf case was absent, a large stone slab adjoining the fireplace held all the family crockery . . . The only bedroom would have a loom in it, a bed or two, and a pair of drawers (Sheeran 1984 Chapter 6).

In some dwellings a small pantry or cellar gave additional food storage space. In single-storey cottages, if either one of these was provided, it was generally an outshut pantry, as at Ratten Row, Lepton (74) and Half Acre Lane, Thornton (134) (Figs 1 and 6). Such outshuts were seldom built on to two-storeyed cottages, the builders of which were more concerned to economize on building land. In two-storeyed dwellings, moreover, the area under the stone stairs could serve as the cool storage space. Cellars occur far more frequently in two- than in one-storeyed cottages, possibly because they added significantly to the cost of building and necessitated the employment of craftsmen with a higher

degree of skill. Where they are found in single-storey cottages it seems that one or more of the factors which led to their provision in two-storey dwellings was responsible. At Waterloo Fold, Wyke (158), for example, cottages were built with their two rooms one behind the other rather than side by side. The adoption of this plan reduced the width of each cottage, so saving on building land. If economizing on land was, indeed, a consideration for the builder in this instance, then it is not surprising that cellars were provided in preference to outshut pantries (Fig 2). Cellars were also provided in the one-roomed cottages at Hudd Hill, Shelf (111) (Fig 4). This row of seven dwellings was built well and of better quality materials than were used in many other single-storey cottages. It seems, therefore, that the person who paid for the cottages was prepared to invest more money in them than was usual for single-storeys. The cottages at both Hudd Hill (111) and Waterloo Fold (158) date to the early 19th century, the period in which cellars began to be provided in single- and two-storeyed cottages. It did not, however, become common for cottages to have cellars until the second quarter of the century.

Cottages which offered more accommodation than simply a living room and bedroom were provided for categories of workers who either had an income sufficiently large to rent them, or skills which employers hoped to attract by building superior dwellings. Cottages of this type often possessed a second ground-floor room, either heated and used as a second living room or parlour (as in Short Row,

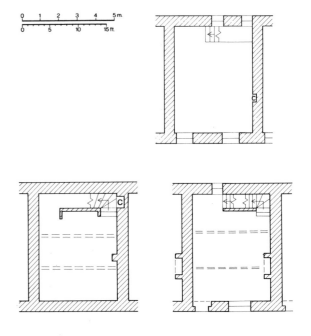

Fig 31. Nos. 6 and 7, Lumb Foot, Stanbury

49

Plate 60. Greenwood Row, Pudsey

Low Moor (101) (Fig 21)), or unheated and functioning as a scullery or a smaller pantry space as at Upper Reins, Honley (57) (Fig 30). Plans of this type were not, however, widely adopted for workers' houses until the early 19th century.

In larger cottages additional sleeping or working room might be provided on the first or second floor, an example of the latter being 437 Manchester Road, Linthwaite (77) (Fig 11). By the late 18th century some contemporaries were expressing the opinion that two bedrooms as well as a living room were essential in order that the male and female children of a family could sleep in separate rooms. Cottage plans prepared by the architects John Wood and Nathaniel Kent in the late 18th century met this minimum requirement (Lowe 1977, 5) and, similarly, competitions held at that time by the Board of Agriculture to promote cottage building stipulated that the plans should provide a living room and two bedrooms (Gauldie 1974, 46).

Cottages which contained more than the basic two rooms were not necessarily larger in floor area than the simpler cottages. The cottages in Bradford Road, Otley (104) were built with a living room, scullery and two bedrooms (Fig 29), but they have almost exactly the same floor area as those built at Lumbfoot, Stanbury (44) (cellar discounted) which had a living room and only one bedroom (Fig 31). In many of the larger cottages the extra space was used as working accommodation. In these cases there was no more actual

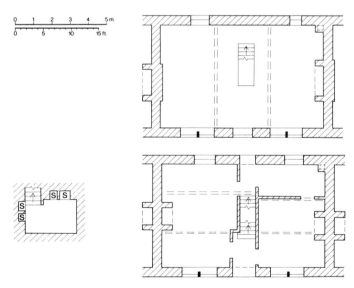

Fig 32. No. 5, Greenwood Row, Pudsey

living room than in smaller cottages that were not used for working in. Many of the double-fronted houses in Pudsey, for example, appear to offer generous accommodation until it is remembered that the upper floors also housed hand-looms. As a consequence the living quarters were in practice reduced to a living room, a scullery and a bedroom (Pl 60, Fig 32). Another example of this are 437–445 Manchester

Plate 61.
Cottages at Low Mill,
Addingham

Road, Linthwaite (77) (Fig 11). The first and second-floor rooms of these were used for working space so that in terms of actual living accommodation they provided no more room than the two-storeyed mill cottages at Low Mill, Addingham (1) (Pl 61). Conversely, other domestic workers, such as the weavers of the Bradford area described c.1830 (see p 000 above), also lived and worked in cottages no larger than those at Low Mill and therefore had even less actual living space. Larger houses were not necessarily better provided with heating than their smaller neighbours. In the basic type of cottage one room only might be heated. More frequently the second room also had a fireplace. Although some of the larger cottages, such as those in Short Row, Low Moor (101) (Fig 21), had several heated rooms it was quite common for there to be only two.

It was in the interest of those who built housing as an investment that their properties should be of sound construction, so as to require a minimum of repairs. A more widespread use of better quality materials was accompanied necessarily by the employment of skilled craftsmen to undertake the building work. Thus, when five cottages in Kirkheaton were repaired in 1749 although various labourers were paid for transporting materials, removing earth etc the largest single items of expenditure were payments to a mason and a carpenter. A glazier and blacksmith were also employed (WYAS Kirklees, Whitley Beaumont Estate Papers 1/22). Some thirty years later, when a tollhouse was built in Highburton, the turnpike trustees employed a mason, a glazier, a carpenter and a carpenter-cum-blacksmith (WYAS, RT42, Halifax and Penistone Turnpike Road). The use of skilled labour would have enabled

buildings of more sophisticated design to be built, a consideration which may have been a factor in the transition from the single- to the two-storey cottage and the emergence of the latter as the dominant form.

In building upwards rather than along savings were made on roofing materials. More important perhaps was the fact that the two-storey plan enabled an equal amount of accommodation to be provided as that in a single-storey cottage, but more compactly, so saving on the cost of land. In areas where building land was particularly expensive or in short supply, not only were two-storeyed cottages built but they took forms which allowed denser development, such as back-to-backs, houses with cellar dwellings beneath them, and the three- or four-storeyed dwellings and underdwellings found in the Pennine valleys.

In the late 18th century stone was the principal walling material. Millstone grit, sandstone or limestone were used according to what was locally available. In some areas the harder and more durable Millstone grit gradually superseded sandstone. Poorer quality dwellings were often built of quarry waste or other cheap stone, in which case thick walls were necessary in order to ensure stability. Walls built of quarry waste were sometimes faced with larger, better-quality blocks of stone, as in the cottage on Half Acre Lane, Thornton (134) (Pl 8). By the early 19th century walls were generally of dressed blocks laid in courses of varying depth which often diminished in depth towards the top of a wall. More skill was required when stone was laid watershot, that is with the stones in the outer face of the wall set at an angle so that the top of each stone overhung its base. This technique had the effect of helping direct water off the surface of the wall. Ashlar, which is found in larger houses, was seldom used at cottage level except when appearance was an important consideration, as in the cottages at Harewood. In this period the principal alternative building material to stone was brick which, although once a prestige building material, was becoming increasingly cheap. It first began to be used for workers' housing in those areas where brick earth was more readily available than building stone, for example in Leeds and Wakefield. In other areas a mixture of brick and stone was used. In many cases while the external walls of houses might still be stone, chimneystacks and internal partitions walls were, increasingly, built of brick.

Permanent materials were also used for roofing. It is apparent from the 1796 Harewood Survey and other documentary sources that thatch was still used in the late 18th and early 19th centuries, but good roofing stone, or thackstone as it was called, was so readily available that generally it was used for all but the most basic structures. By 1822 all the farmhouses, cottages and other buildings of Little Lepton had slate roofs, including the outbuildings (with the exception of one cowhouse) and the three single-roomed parish poor cottages, which were the lowest status dwellings in the hamlet and said to be in 'very bad repair' (WBE/153 Redmonds). The Harewood Survey indicates that tile was sometimes used as a roofing material (Survey 1796, 127), but such examples are rare.

This period also brought a change in building materials and the way in which they were used within the cottages. Softwood was imported to England in increasing quantities from the late 18th century and, being cheaper, it began to replace the locally available hardwood in even the humbler workers' dwellings. In West Yorkshire this change was initiated by the development of the canal system. Softwood was being used in the Colne Valley, served by the Huddersfield Narrow Canal, by the late 18th century, but did not arrive in the more remote Holme Valley until the early 19th century (D Michelmore pers comm).

Since they were easier to cut and shape softwood timbers were generally more slender and better-finished than the large-scantling, frequently crooked and crudely-shaped timbers which they superseded. There were developments also in the type of roof truss employed, the queen post with raking struts becoming more common. This form was particularly suitable for use when the roof was of a wide span, as in the back-to-backs at Thongsbridge (90), built in 1790; but was also used for narrower buildings such as 437 Manchester Road, Linthwaite (77) (Fig 11). Not every cottage made use of a roof truss, and in many it was deemed sufficient to support the purlins solely on the gable and party walls, a type of roof structure which was both simpler and cheaper to construct, although not as strong. As well as

being provided with better built walls and roofs, cottages of this period were given more permanent floor surfaces. Stone flags were laid in ground-floor rooms and on the floors of living-rooms in upper dwellings, in these cases usually over boards. Other rooms had timber floors, narrower softwood boards gradually replacing broader ones of hardwood.

Certain general provisions were common to all cottages of this period regardless of size and type. Access, for example, was generally given by only one door, and this opened directly into the living room. After the turn of the 18th century back doors were occasionally provided in the larger houses, as in the cottages on Main Street, Burley-in-Wharfedale (16) (Fig 28). Sometimes a wooden spere projected into the room beside the doorway, reducing the draught to a certain extent (see for example Fig 30), but in many cases these will have been inserted later. Occasionally original doors have survived. Internal ones were made of vertical boards battened with simple wooden or iron latches, like that in the clothier's house at Ryecroft (19) (Pl 62).

Plate 62. Farmhouse at Ryecroft, near Holmfirth: door

Plate 63. No.2, Green Bower, Marsden: door

Plate 64. Dairy window, No.90, Main Street, Burley in Wharfedale

External doors often had four recessed panels on the front with a backing of vertical boards like the door to No 2 Green Bower, Marsden (87) which still has its original latch, bolts and lock (Pl 63). The specifications for a toll cottage built in 1805 were for similar doors, the

> Out Doors inch and quarter (315 mm) boards well batted outside with Lock and Handle: In Doors with checks good half inch (130 mm) deals
>
> (WYAS Wakefield, RT94)

Windows also came in standardized forms. In some cottages, even those which were not built back-to-earth, there were no openings at all in the back wall, presumably to cut down on heat-loss and the expense of glazing where the

extra light could be dispensed with. In larger houses the Window Tax levied between 1696 and 1851 was responsible in some cases for causing windows to be blocked or kept to a minimum.

Although the smaller cottages would not usually have enough windows to make them eligible for taxation, the Window Tax has left its mark. Tax did not have to be paid on windows to rooms which were not lived in, such as dairies and pantries. To prevent these windows being included by the assessors they were labelled as such, the larder windows of two of the cottages in Main Street, Burley-in-Wharfedale (16), for example, have retained their sign 'Dairy' (Pl 64)[1]. Workers' cottages were generally provided with windows that were divided into several lights

53

Plate 65. Window types used in the late 18th and early 19th centuries:
(a) Bridge end, Mytholmroyd; (b) No. 1, St. Mary's Court, Honley; (c) Town Street, Armley; (d) Wormald Yard, Huddersfield

by mullions, although their exact form often followed chronological and local variations (Pl 65). Hung sash windows made their appearance in larger houses in the 18th century, and by the end of it vertical or horizontal sliding sashes were provided in the smaller cottages, although the sashes were not hung and would have been wedged open.

The earliest windows were formed of small panes of glass, like those which survive in the late 18th-century cottages in Wormald Yard, Huddersfield (63) (Pl 65d). When windows were larger in area and undivided by mullions, a small portion of the window was made to open as a casement (Pl 65a). Sometimes a window was designed so as to provide a window seat by lowering the inside cill or not building it up at all, an arrangement used in the living-rooms of Club Row, Wilsden (155) and Upper Reins, Honley (57).

Builders also made use of the thickness of walls to provide recessed cupboards or shelves. These were common in cellars, but were also made in the rooms above (see Figs 30, 31) for where cottage walls were thick it was a simple matter to leave a recess without endangering the walls' stability. Recessed cupboards were superseded by wall cupboards formed by partitioning of a portion of the room, generally in line with the chimney breast. Stone was used within cottages to provide shelving, particularly in the cellars, scullery and pantry areas, and also for sinks. Arrangements for the provision of a water supply were generally left to the inhabitants themselves. In most cases water was collected

Plate 66. Spring at Green End, Old Town

from a communal spring, well or pump (Pl 66). In some of the dwellings visited there were originally wells in the cellars, for example in the cottages in Barber Row, Linthwaite (76).

In this period cottagers also seem to have been left to their own devices as regards the provision of privies. There is some evidence of these having been provided. The toll cottage built at Lightcliffe in 1805, for example, was to have 'a convenient necessary house', and early plans of the lock cottages at Brookfoot (108) and Elland Middle Lock (36) show that what has been enlarged into a wash-kitchen was originally a small, square outbuilding enclosed by a yard – probably a privy of some sort (British Waterways Board 1734). A similar outbuilding is shown in the plans of other Calder and Hebble Navigation Company cottages (British Waterways Board 1834). In an outbuilding at Wellhouse Field, Golcar (41) there were three pail privies, which appear to have been provided when the six cottages were built, c.1830.[2] It may be that the physical evidence of privies from this period has now disappeared, the privies having become inadequate and been replaced by later conveniences. On the other hand they may have been uncommon at that time. The Harewood Survey of 1796 mentions yards and coal-pits, but no 'necessaries' or privies. Later, in the mid-19th century, commentators were to deplore the lack of privies and the inadequacies of existing ones.

Back yards were provided for some cottages, like those at Harewood (Survey 1796) where they housed coal-sheds and other buildings. Elsewhere, although there was an area behind the cottages, yards were not built as an original feature; at others, like Kenmore, Ryecroft (18), farmland originally ran up to the rear wall of the cottage so as to leave no room for a back area of any sort.

Another provision about which commentators felt more strongly was that cottagers should have an allotment or piece of ground which could be cultivated. In the textile industry it had long been customary for clothiers to also be engaged in husbandry. In the course of the 18th century cloth manufacture became increasingly the most important element in this dual economy, nonetheless agriculture continued to provide many with a supplementary means of income. Writing in 1799, Robert Brown observed that:

> in the vicinity of the manufacturing towns [Bradford, Halifax, Huddersfield and Leeds] . . . The greatest part of the ground is there occupied by persons who do not consider farming as a business, but regard it only as a matter of convenience. The manufacturer has his enclosure, wherein he keeps milch cows for supporting his family, and horses for carrying his goods to market, and bringing back raw materials (Brown 1799, 77–78).

In the early 19th century many cottages continued to practise a dual economy, albeit to a limited extent. Domestic textile workers were not alone in their practising of spade husbandry. At Bowling iron works, for example, 'iron was only made in six months in the year . . . the men filling up the remainder of the year in the way they best could' (Cudworth 1891, 231). It is probable that some of these workers were involved in part-time spade husbandry. The Low Moor Iron Company's houses at Short Row, North Bierley (101) were provided with long strips to the rear, which must have been designed as allotments for the tenants. Even for those who did not practice a dual economy it was generally believed a good idea for a cottage to have land attached, so that the occupant could keep a cow or pig or grow crops, which would not only cushion him from fluctuating food prices and help him through periods of unemployment or hardship, but by doing so would also reduce the number of destitute labourers who had to rely on parish relief (Brown 1799, 15). At Harewood, where the villagers were 'principally composed of farmers, shopkeepers, artisans and labourers' (Jewell 1819, 12), the estate surveyors remarked that

> It was . . . a great satisfaction to us to find on going over this part of the Estate that great Indulgence has been shown to the Inhabitants of Harewood in letting them have small Parcels of Land to keep a Cow or two – A mode of letting which we hope will never be superseded (Survey 1796, 108)

This tradition of part-time husbandry continued into the 19th century.

Notes to Chapter 3
[1] Although these signs have been touched-up over the years, they appear to be original features.
[2] These were set in a line down one side of a shed adjoining the barn. The floor level in the other half of the shed was lower, and from it the pails beneath the wooden toilet seats could be removed and emptied.

CHAPTER 4

THE CHANGING SCALE OF INDUSTRY

TEXTILES

The textile industry continued to be the single most important element in West Yorkshire's economy in the 1850s. The trend towards larger, more centralized units of production resulted in the disappearance of all but a handful of the small independent clothiers who had for so long predominated in the industry as it had been organised in the county. The transition from domestic to factory production was, however, a gradual one. The 1851 and 1861 censuses show that a substantial number of weavers were still working at hand-looms, the majority in their own homes (censuses eg Shelf 1851; Glover 1959, 185).

Domestic hand-loom weaving survived longest in the woollen areas, since it was not until the 1850s that a reliable power-loom for the weaving of woollens was developed. Hand-loom weaving was still commonly practiced in the woollen-district villages near Leeds and in the Huddersfield area until the 1870s and '80s (Glover 1959, 188). A journalist examining the condition of the working-class of the manufacturing districts in 1849 found that in Batley Carr 'the weaving is, for the most part, carried on at the homes of the workpeople', while at Paddock, Huddersfield, 'looms

invariably occupied the first floor' (cited by Ward 1970, 163). As late as 1881 a Pudsey newspaper advertised:

> To let, a house at Balloon Row, Intake Row. Two large rooms on the ground floor; chamber over all will hold three broad looms; two cellars; gas fittings in every room; plenty of outside conveniences (*Pudsey and Stanningley News* 29 April 1881, reference supplied by R Strong).

In the fancy-goods branch of the textile industry hand-loom weaving could not be bettered by power-looms, and in some areas, as at Outlane, Huddersfield, and in Skelmanthorpe, domestic weaving continued into the 1920s, a late example of purpose-built weavers' cottages being a terrace of eleven houses with provision for hand-looms, built in Skelmanthorpe in 1903. Some of the earlier cottages of these fancy weavers were affected in this period by the introduction into West Yorkshire of jacquard looms in the 1820s.[1] These looms, used for the weaving of patterned cloth were taller than those they replaced, so necessitating, in some cases, the heightening of cottage roofs. This feature is to be seen in several of the dwellings in the Skelmanthorpe area (Pls 67, 68).

Plate 67.
Weavers' cottages with raised roofs in Skelmanthorpe

Plate 68 (*left*).
Weavers' cottages, Skelmanthorpe:
gable end, showing roof heightening

Plate 69 (*right*).
Weavers' cottages, Golcar, 1845

Plate 70. Reconstructed interior of weaver's cottage, Golcar

Weavers' cottages continued to be built in the 1840s and '50s (Pls 69, 70). After the middle of the century, however, the decline in the number of hand-loom weavers reduced demand for housing of this kind. As a result most weavers were able to find accommodation within the existing housing stock. That this was the case is illustrated by the many advertisements in local papers which sought tenants or purchasers for houses that had been used for hand-loom weaving, such as that in Pudsey quoted above.

The continued growth in the average size of mills, both in terms of fixed capital invested and in the workforces employed, was paralleled by the building of larger and larger housing developments to house the growing work-force of the industry. Typical of this process was the Mallinson's family business in Linthwaite, the expansion of which in the second half of the 19th century was mirrored by its provision of housing on an increasingly ambitious scale. In 1852 the Mallinsons built Myrtle Grove (79), a terrace of thirteen cottages, which was over twice the length of Barber Row, a terrace of six cottages built by them earlier in the century (76) and had considerably more architectural embellishment, although the cottages themselves were of a

Plate 71 (*above*).
Barber Row, Linthwaite

similar size (compare Pls 71 and 72). A similar illustration of the growth in a mill workforce is provided by the housing at Highgate Mill, Clayton. The earliest dwellings associated with this are a row of four cottages facing into the mill-yard of *c*.1849 (22). In 1865 a further eighteen cottages were built in a row adjoining the owner's house (23). These cottages flank an archway, the monumental nature of which is a further reflection of the growing prosperity and self-confidence of the textile industry as a whole (Pl 73). Another example, on an even larger scale, was the Ripley dyeworks in Bradford. This venture expanded from a workforce of only eighteen men and boys in 1821, to one of 1000 seventy years later (Cudworth 1891, 246, 248). In the 1860s Henry Ripley built several streets of houses, known locally as Ripleyville, to accommodate them (Cudworth 1891, 249).

In the second half of the 19th century, the textile industry was responsible for producing some of the most outstanding housing developments of the age. Between 1849 and 1853 Edward Akroyd built 112 back-to-backs for his workers, close to his mill at Copley (Pl 74). This housing was augmented, subsequently, by the building of twenty-four through houses. More ambitious still was his creation of the settlement of Akroydon, near Halifax, in the years 1861 to

Plate 72 (*left*).
Myrtle Grove, Linthwaite

Plate 73 (*above*).
Highgate Mill, Clayton

Plate 74 (*left*).
Akroyd's housing
at Copley

Plate 75 (*left*).
Beverley Terrace,
Akroydon

Plate 76 (*below*).
Ripon Terrace,
Akroydon

'68, which involved the building of some 350 houses, carefully planned around an open square (*Builder* 1863, 109–11) (Pls 75–81). A similarly large development was undertaken by the Crossleys of Dean Clough Mills, Halifax, in the West Hill Park area of the town (1863–68) (Pls 82–5). The largest and best known of the mill housing developments in West Yorkshire, however, was Saltaire, Shipley, where, by 1860, Titus Salt had built some 450 houses for the workers in his alpaca mill (*Builder* 1860, 49; Reynolds 1983, 256–325) (Pls 86–8).

Plate 77. Salisbury Place, Akroydon

Plate 78. Ripon Terrace, Akroydon

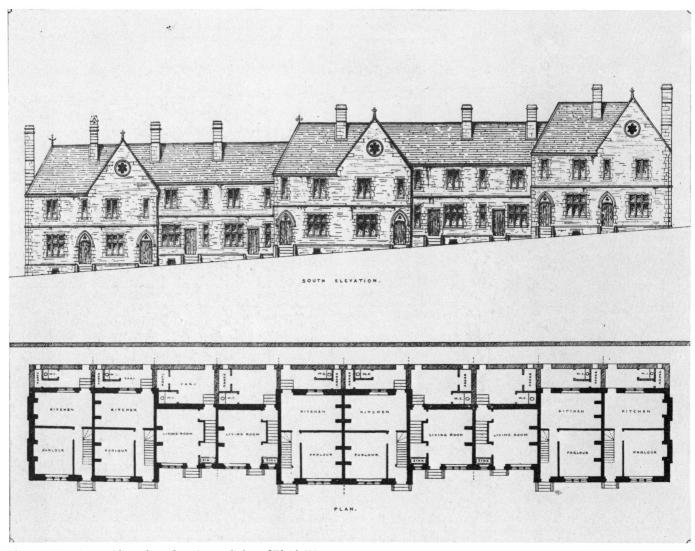

SOUTH ELEVATION.

PLAN.

Plate 79. Housing at Akroydon: elevation and plan of Block IV

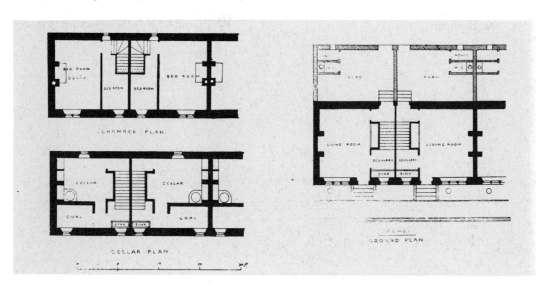

CHAMBER PLAN.

CELLAR PLAN

GROUND PLAN

Plate 80 (*left*).
Housing at Akroydon:
plan of Block II

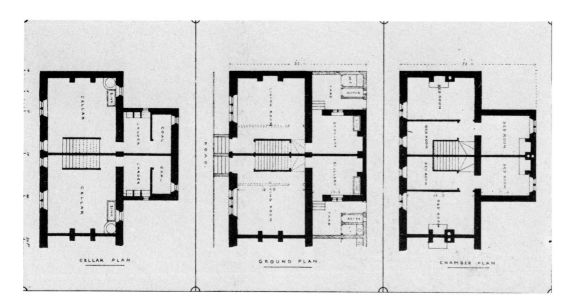

CELLAR PLAN.

GROUND PLAN.

CHAMBER PLAN.

Plate 80a (*left*).
Housing at Akroydon:
plan of Block III

Plate 81 (*below*).
Akroydon: artist's
impression of the
development as conceived

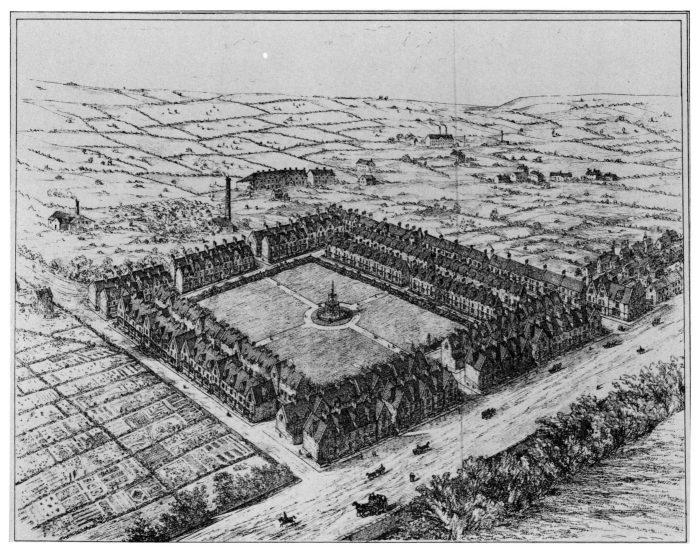

Plate 82 (*above*).
West Hill Park, Halifax:
artist's impression of
the development as
conceived

Plate 83 (*right*).
Gilbert Street, West Hill Park

Plate 84 (*above*).
West Hill Street,
West Hill Park

Plate 85 (*left*).
Grosvenor Terrace,
West Hill Park

Plate 86 (*left*).
Lockwood Road, Saltaire

Plate 87 (*right*).
Albert Road, Saltaire

Plate 88 (*left*).
Caroline Street,
Saltaire

Plate 89 (*left*).
Holme Villas, Lingards

Fig 33 (*below*).
Holme Villas, Lingards

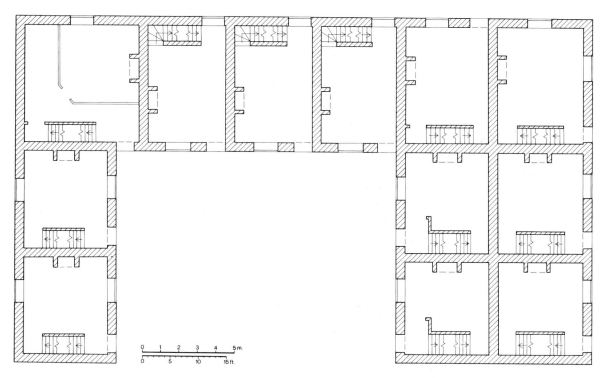

A number of more modest schemes were undertaken by smaller employers in this period. In 1873 Cook, Hague and Wormalds, for example, built thirty back-to-back and six through cottages at Dewsbury Mills. At much the same time William Leigh Brook provided forty-one houses for his mill-workers at Royd Edge, Meltham. Adjoining New Mills, Marsden, is a terrace of twenty-eight back-to-backs built in 1879. There are other developments, many of which are even smaller, such as the courts of twelve dwellings at Holme Villas, Lingards (1864) (Pl 89; Fig 33), and at Wilshaw (1873) (Pl 90).

Some of those employers who were building workers' housing in this period were motivated, not only by the need to provide accommodation, but also by a sense of responsibility and moral obligation to their employees. These considerations certainly influenced the character of the

Plate 90.
St. Mary's Court,
Wilshaw

textile housing provided at Copley, Akroydon, West Hill Park and Saltaire. The philanthropic motive gave an added dimension to house-building, for employers then had in mind the welfare of the prospective tenants. Without such considerations housing was often built following the most basic contemporary house-plans and standards. The second-phase cottages at Highgate Mill, Clayton (23), and those in Myrtle Grove, Linthwaite (79), for example, consisted of only a living-room with a bedroom above. Accommodation of this standard was no advance on that offered fifty years previously. Nonetheless, because it represented part of a fixed capital investment, whether there was an element of philanthropic motivation or not, housing provided by employers was generally well built.

THE EXTRACTIVE INDUSTRIES

In the extractive industries, as in textiles, this period was one of transition from small ventures to larger, more capitally intensive concerns. In the west of the county a number of small quarries and coal-pits continued to operate. In these areas the traditional forms of housing associated with the industry persisted. At Grange Moor, for example, single-storey cottages continued to be built, one row as late as the last quarter of the 19th century. In North Bierley the Low Moor Iron Company dominated the local economy, but, despite the considerable size of this venture, small-scale developments of single-storey dwellings continued to be built for much of its workforce. A report on miners' conditions, published in 1845, complained that such cottages were of 'insufficient size and inconvenient arrangement for a decent family' (Report on Mining Population 1845, cited by Mee 1975, 141). It seems, however, that in this area, where the single-storey cottage was a firmly-established type, it continued to be built for the less affluent workers.[2]

The most significant trend in coal mining in this period was an increasing concentration of the industry in the east of the county where continued technological advances made it possible to sink shafts to work the deeper and thicker seams of this part of the coalfield. Increasingly large sums of capital were needed to enable mining to be undertaken on a scale sufficiently large to allow operational economies. The need to raise and command considerable amounts of capital resulted in small family firms gradually being supplanted by larger limited companies (Lewis 1971, 41; Goodchild 1976, 6–13; Goodchild 1977, 4). These concerns required increasingly large workforces, resulting in competition for labour and for skilled workers in particular, who often came from other coalfields. Pope and Pierson's Colliery at Altofts hired workers from Derbyshire, Gloucestershire, Leicestershire, Staffordshire, Warwickshire, Worcestershire and Ireland, but few from Yorkshire (Goodchild 1977, 6). In order to attract miners to their collieries employers built the sizeable housing developments characteristic of the industry in the second half of the century. At Altofts the miners were housed in fifty-two three-storeyed cottages in Silkstone Row, with a shorter row of seven cottages for higher status employees. This necessity to attract labour by providing accommodation is also illustrated by a proposal made in 1866 by the board of the colliery company Henry Briggs Son and Co Ltd.

That the Secretary and managers be recommended to make early arrangements for building by contract or otherwise, at least one hundred cottages; in order to obtain more hands and increase the business of the company (University of Leeds MS 160, 67).

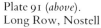

Plate 91 (*above*).
Long Row, Nostell

Plate 92 (*left*).
Long Row,
New Sharlston

Nearly as extensive as Pope and Pierson's Silkstone Row was Long Row, Nostell (37). This comprised forty-seven cottages built in 1860 and 1865 by Charles Winn for miners employed at the Nostell Priory estate colliery (Taylor 1978, 119) (Pl 91). The Charlesworths, owners of a number of mines in the Lofthouse and Rothwell area, also built several terraces of cottages, including Brighteyes Row, Lofthouse, and Angel Row, Rothwell Haigh, both *c*.1860 (Goodchild 1978, 70). After the formation of the New Sharlston Colliery Company in 1864, this concern, too, built large numbers of cottages near their pit. One of their terraces, Long Row, New Sharlston (110) consisted of twenty-nine through cottages and twenty-six back-to-backs (Pl 92). Other houses were built in Crossley Street and High Street (Goodchild 1976, 11, 20) and by the 1890s the company owned 174 houses in this settlement.[3]

The housing built by these colliery companies stands out from earlier cottages in being built, typically, of brick roofed with thin grey slate. These materials were used as much for economic reasons as any other. Fireclay was often dug from the mines and, when made into bricks, was used for lining shafts, for pit-head buildings and for miners' housing. Some companies ran their own brickworks, as at Nostell, where the estate owners opened a brickworks next to the colliery in 1875 (Taylor 1978, 119). Other companies contracted out this work, amongst them the New Sharlston Colliery Company. This concern started a brickworks in the 1860s, during the sinking of new shafts, and the bricks produced were used extensively in the colliery buildings (Goodchild 1976, 18). The thin slate used so extensively as a roofing material for miners' housing was imported from Wales, its cheapness enabling it to compete favourably with local roofing stone despite the cost of transportation. In the case of the colliery companies, moreover, transport was not a problem, since the slate could be brought in by the same railways that carried out their coal.

THE COMING OF THE RAILWAYS

One of the most significant developments of the period was the building of the national railway system, an important consequence of which was the great stimulus it gave to further industrial growth. In West Yorkshire the first line to be laid was the Leeds to Selby railway, opened in 1834. This was followed in 1840 by the opening of a line from Leeds to Manchester and one from Derby to York, a branch line of the latter railway running from Normanton to Leeds. Activity intensified in the 1840s, in which decade numerous other main and branch lines were constructed (Haigh 1978, 7–8). These railways were built and operated by a number of companies, the majority of which were to disappear as the result of amalgamations and take-overs which took place in the second half of the century. By the late 19th century the railway network of West Yorkshire was dominated by the Great Northern, the Lancashire and Yorkshire, the London and North Western, the Midland, and the North Eastern Railway Companies (Haigh 1978, 9–10).

These larger companies all provided a certain amount of employee accommodation. In the 1840s housing was built for railway workers at Normanton, then an important junction on the route north,[4] including a terrace of thirteen houses next to the railway sidings (Goodchild 1975, 10; Ordnance Survey 1:2500 Map). The majority of railway housing in Normanton was not, however, built until the 1870s and '80s. This is true, also, of much of the railway housing in the county, which, for the most part, was built by the larger companies in the later 19th century. It seems that the smaller companies, with less capital available and

employing comparatively small numbers of railway workers, had neither the means nor the incentive to provide accommodation for their employees. The later, larger, companies were in a somewhat different position. The Midland Railway Company was one which provided housing on a large scale. At Normanton in 1875, for example, a contractor, Robert Leake, completed the building of thirty-seven houses for them, along with stabling for horses and other outbuildings (Goodchild 1975, 10). By 1880 the Midland had had another substantial housing development built at Bradford consisting of forty houses facing into the company's shunting yard (Pls 93, 94; Fig 43). (This terrace is very similar in appearance to other railway housing in Normanton, now demolished (Andreae 1950, 179).) The Bradford houses were occupied by company employees, mostly engine-drivers but also some less-skilled workers, including a labourer and a plate-layer (Directory 1880). The Lancashire and Yorkshire Railway Company, like the Midland, provided housing for employees next to their shunting yard at Low Moor, Bradford.

Railway houses were built in smaller groups when fewer workers were employed. The terrace along the railway line at Outwood, Wakefield (128), comprises seven houses built c.1880 for railwaymen working at the nearby station and signal box. Houses were often built singly at level-crossings over the lines, these being occupied rent-free, in return for which the tenant minded the gates (PRO Rail 527/952). Cottages were also built in groups of four along the railways, as at Garforth (38), in order to house the plate-layers who worked in small gangs along sections of the line.

Railway cottages were very different to much other contemporary housing. The transportation of materials presented no difficulties for the railway companies, making it economical for them to build houses from materials brought in from outside the county. As a result railway housing, like that of miners, was characteristically built of brick with roofs of thin Welsh slate, although there are some examples built of local stone.

One reason for railway companies providing accommodation was their belief that in so doing they would improve the quality of the workforce. In 1861 the Board of the Great Northern Railway was told that

> the value to the Company of having their servants comfortably located and near to their work must be great, as it must improve the class of servants working for us (PRO Rail 236/286(14).[5]

It would, moreover, cost the company very little to avail themselves of this benefit, 'cottages with such certain tenants, and such easy means of getting paid [ie deduction of rent from wages], can easily be built to pay a fair percentage'

Plate 93 (*above*).
Midland Terrace,
Bradford

Plate 94 (*left*).
Midland Terrace,
Bradford: two houses

Plate 95. Railway housing, Outwood, Wakefield

Plate 96. Outwood, Wakefield:
detail of porch

Plate 97 (*left*).
Railway housing, Batley

(*ibid*). Once the workforce was accommodated in company housing its quality in the eyes of the employer could be further enhanced by its enforced compliance, for recalcitrant workers could be disciplined with the threat of eviction. Apart from the imposition of discipline, employers doubtless found that, by accommodating their workers in well-built, sanitary houses, they improved their employees' health, and so their reliability and regularity (Gauldie 1974, 187–90). Housing could simultaneously also act as a display of wealth, prestige and philanthropy of the companies that built them and considerations of this kind may well have been responsible for the architectural quality and lavish detail displayed in much railway housing (Pls 95, 96, 97).

Notes to Chapter 4

[1] The earliest known use of jacquard looms in West Yorkshire is at Edward Akroyd's Halifax mills where they were installed in 1827 (Bretton 1948, 67).
[2] See for example the Wool-combers' Report (Bradford Sanitary Committee 1845) and the Halifax Corporation Health Committee Minute Books (1848–71).
[3] It is interesting that company philanthropy was practised at New Sharlston to a greater extent than was done by most other colliery companies. This is likely to have been the result of the involvement of the Crossleys as partners in the company (Goodchild 1976, 8–11), for in Halifax the Crossley brothers were deeply involved in the provision of housing, institutions and other facilities for their textile workers (Linstrum and Powell 1977, 14–15).
[4] The North Midland Railway Company's line from Leeds to Derby, the York and North Midlands' line from Normanton to York, and the Manchester and Leeds Railway's line all met here (Goodchild 1977, a).
[5] In 1885 the Metropolitan Railway had also found the result of providing housing 'very beneficial, both to the railway and to the workmen' (Parliamentary Papers 1885, p. 460 12,625).

CHAPTER 5

SPECULATION AND SELF-HELP

SPECULATORS

The urban population of West Yorkshire continued to expand rapidly in the second half of the 19th century. The rate of increase in Bradford between 1851 and 1881 was as high as 79 per cent (Lumb 1951, 8). In the county's other industrial towns growth continued at a dramatic, if not so spectacular, rate, the population of Leeds, for example, increasing by 49,000 between 1871 and 1881 (Royal Commission on Housing 1884, 326, S9787). The ever-increasing demand for accommodation which this expansion engendered made house-building a profitable industry in its own right, and one in which the speculative builder was quick to become involved. More is known about their activities from this time than earlier in the century because of the increased scope of documentary records, including such valuable sources as building plans, trade directories and contemporary reports.

Some of those who speculated in housing did so as a side-interest.[1] The majority, however, were first and foremost engaged in the building trade. Many of them were listed in the trade directories as builders or architects and, when they were not themselves architects, they seem to have employed members of that profession to draw their plans.[2] These builders derived their income, together with the capital to invest in further housing schemes, from the money they made through selling off newly completed houses, rather than from renting them out.

Speculative builders of the mid- and late 19th century were extremely active in urban areas. The process of infilling and redeveloping central yards and courts continued. In Leeds, for example, 37 St Peter's Square was subdivided into four dwellings c.1849 and in the yard behind the house the owner erected three new cottages (LPBS Surveyors Book 1851–2, 327). Of much greater significance, however, was the development of what had previously been agricultural land beyond the urban centres. In Bradford the area north of Leeds Road is just one such part of the city which was developed in this way. Gladstone and Amberley Streets, for example, were built up in the 1860s and '70s, the same builders being active in both these and other streets in the area. Thomas Peel built thirteen houses in Gladstone Street in 1871 and another nine two

years later. John Dobson added his quota of seven in 1875 and the following year built twenty-six back-to-backs in Amberley Street, after which he appears to have gone into partnership with a Mr. Lear (WYAS BF Building Plans, Index). Development, here and elsewhere, became even more intense in the following decade and, true to the trend observed in the enterprises of other builders, was made on a large scale (*ibid*).

In expanding urban areas land was, then as now, a valuable commodity, being in demand for the construction of industrial and commercial premises as well as for house-building. Its cost encouraged speculators seeking to maximize profits to build as densely as possible. The house plan which speculative builders adopted in these urban areas for workers' housing was, therefore, invariably the back-to-back.

Elsewhere, the same desire to produce 'a maximum of rent for a minimum of outlay' (Bradford 1864, 9) encouraged the further development of earlier house plans that had made maximum use of difficult building ground. This was particularly the case in those towns situated in the Pennine uplands, where flat building land was in short supply. In Holmfirth, for example the dwelling-and-underdwelling plan was used for a terrace of six dwellings built along Dunford Road (157) between 1863 and 1865 (Fig 34). The underdwellings in this development were built with a second storey, making them larger and the block taller than earlier versions of the plan-type. These dwellings were built up against an earlier block, access to the underdwellings being given by means of a passage which ran beneath the ground floor of the upper dwelling. In this way, the builder saved both on the land that would have been needed to make this block free-standing and on the materials that would have been needed to build the gable wall had use not been made of the existing, adjoining gable wall. Even more economic use was made of land in the building of a longer terrace some ten years later at Eastwood, Sowerby (124), along the River Calder. In this development a single-storeyed underdwelling was surmounted by a pair of back-to-backs, the rear one of which was reached by means of a balcony running the length of the terrace (Pls 98, 99, Fig 35). Other similar terraces were built in the Calder Valley,

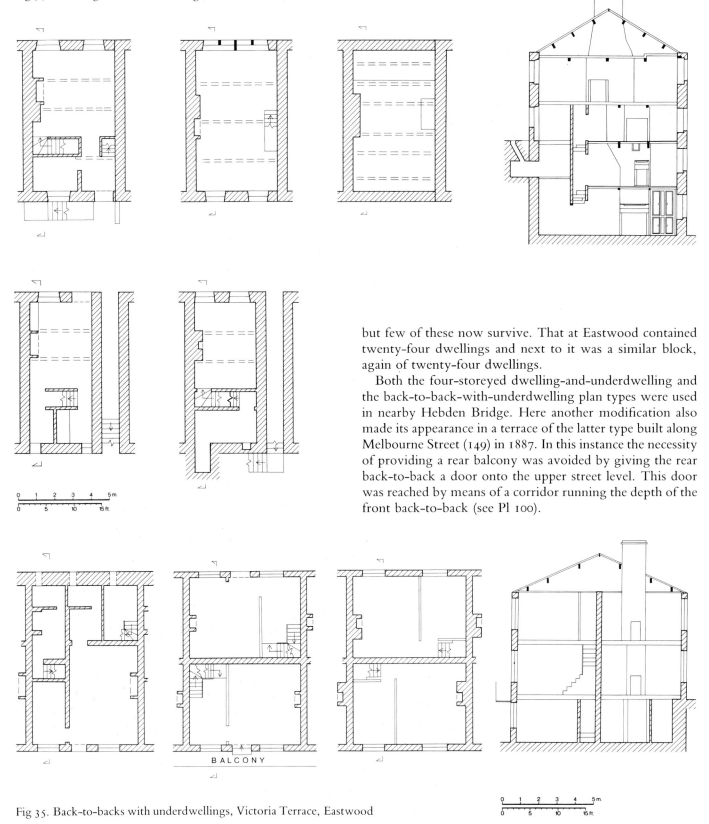

Fig 34. Dwellings and underdwellings, Dunford Road, Holmfirth

but few of these now survive. That at Eastwood contained twenty-four dwellings and next to it was a similar block, again of twenty-four dwellings.

Both the four-storeyed dwelling-and-underdwelling and the back-to-back-with-underdwelling plan types were used in nearby Hebden Bridge. Here another modification also made its appearance in a terrace of the latter type built along Melbourne Street (149) in 1887. In this instance the necessity of providing a rear balcony was avoided by giving the rear back-to-back a door onto the upper street level. This door was reached by means of a corridor running the depth of the front back-to-back (see Pl 100).

BALCONY

Fig 35. Back-to-backs with underdwellings, Victoria Terrace, Eastwood

Plate 98 (*left*).
Back-to-backs with
underdwellings,
Victoria Terrace,
Eastwood

Plate 99 (*right*).
Victoria Terrace,
Eastwood:
gable-end, showing levels

Plate 100.
Back-to-back with
underdwellings,
Melbourne Street,
Hebden Bridge

Speculators were governed almost entirely by economic considerations, the standards of the houses they built being dictated both by the desire to make the best possible return on capital outlay and by the price people were prepared to pay. In many cases the result was houses similar to those in the Haley Hill area of Halifax, which in the 1850s were said to be

> generally speaking . . . of an inferior class, inconvenient and ill ventilated and for the most part only a single living-room and chamber, however numerous may be the inmates. Until lately they were badly drained and without any supply of water – hence typhus and fever found its usual haunts and victims (*Builder* 1863, 109).

Although the design and facilities of this type of property were criticized, it was not necessarily these factors so much as the location of the housing which created the greatest problems, and which exacerbated its other failings. Edward Akroyd, the writer of this comment, had himself, only ten years previously, built houses at Copley as one-up/one-down back-to-backs. Copley was, however, situated in a rural location: there was plenty of fresh air circulating freely and inadequate sanitation was probably not so noticeable. The worst fault of certain speculative housing was, then, the density at which it was built rather than its design and construction.

THE PERMANENT BUILDING SOCIETIES

Towards the middle of the century the building club and terminating building society began to give way to the

Plate 101. Plaque on Friendly Society (Oddfellows) housing, Skelmanthorpe

permanent building society (Pl 101). Unlike the terminating societies, which were wound up once all the founder members were housed, the permanent ones, as their name implies, continually admitted new members. The large number of societies which registered their rules under the Building Societies Act of 1836 bears witness to the strength of the movement in West Yorkshire, many new societies being founded between the 1830s and 50s. A number of permanent building societies grew out of freehold land societies founded in the late 1840s. The object of these latter was to make it possible for working men to acquire a house and land in order to qualify for a vote in parliamentary elections for county seats, since, following the Reform Act of 1832, one property qualification for the vote was a freehold with a rateable value of 40s *per annum*. The Bradford Benefit Building Society, founded in 1849, for example, announced that its 'leading object' was to enable members to buy land and build houses, 'by which they become entitled to a vote for the county' (Bradford Benefit Building Society 1852, vii). An advertisement for the Bradford Equitable Building Society and Freehold Land Society was even more explicit:

Working men of Bradford – of England! To you the Committee appeal. Your own enfranchisement is within your reach. Be independent and noble minded (cited by Gaskell 1971, 159).

By 1853 it was said of Halifax that

. . . for political purposes many men . . . had already become freeholders; building houses with the assistance of the Halifax Union Building Society (*Builder* 1863, 109).

Understandably, then, there was some disquiet when, in 1855, a Court of Appeal ruled that building society mortgages were not an eligible qualification for a county vote and the Leeds Permanent Building Society was not alone in protesting against this decision (Leeds Permanent 1948, 13).

By 1855, however, the commercial value of the building societies had become apparent. The temporary building societies had a number of inherent deficiencies which could and did lead to the failure of building schemes. Not only were members of terminating societies free to leave them when they wished, taking with them their subscriptions and so leaving the society short of funds, but there were also problems caused through inexperience, which led societies to underestimate building costs, or become easy victims of fraud. Within a short time of their establishment, the commercial success of the permanent building societies began to outweigh political considerations and they continued to flourish and expand. The political element appears to have disappeared entirely from the Leeds Permanent Benefit Building Society by 1884, in which year the Chairman reported that its object was

To offer facilities to the working classes for purchasing their own dwellings, and also to encourage and find investment for small savings (Royal Commission on Housing 1884, 371, S10786).

The building societies lent money to all categories of builder. The borrowers of the smallest amounts were often members of the working classes who wished to buy their own houses. It was to people of this category that the Leeds Permanent sought to lend money. Although in 1884 the Chairman felt that originally the Society was 'more a working-class society than we are at the present time' (Royal Commission on Housing 1884, 376, S10,869), it could number amongst its mortgagers at that time millhands, iron-workers, labourers, domestic servants and workers of other occupations (*ibid*, 377, S10,878–80). In 1851 three colliers, David, John and Elijah Fox, borrowed money to build three cottages and a single-storey shop (LPBS Surveyor's Book 1851, 282). Another miner, William Lee, it is recorded, built a pair of similar cottages at the same time (*ibid*, 347). It was borrowers like these that the Leeds Society wished to encourage and in 1884 it was stated that,

we should, had we sufficient applications advance the whole of our money for working-class cottages (Royal Commission on Housing 1884, 371, S10,787).

One difficulty for lower-paid house-buyers was to qualify for a loan by putting down an initial deposit, which generally consisted of about a quarter of the cost of the property. Only where no initial deposit was required, as with the Halifax Building Society (Gauldie 1974, 202), and when repayment could be made over a period of twenty years (Gauldie 1974, 203), could lower-paid workers take on a building society loan. By the late 19th century many building societies' requirements excluded less affluent workers from membership. Borrowers from the Bradford Equitable Building Society and Freehold Land Society (Pls 102–3), for example, were largely foremen, clerks, schoolmasters, shopkeepers and the like and in one of the society's developments, at Salt Street in 1861, only one house-holder, a millhand, was in a lower-income category (Gaskell 1971, 160–1).

It was not unusual for borrowers to build more than a single house. Compared to other building societies, the Leeds Permanent had a large proportion of single-house owners amongst its customers – 25 per cent (Royal Commission on Housing 1884, 375, S 10,838), but even this society lent to many small-scale investors who owned more than one house, for,

> if a person wants his own house he finds it cheaper to build two, three, or four houses and live in one of them himself and let the other three off (ibid, 372, S10,816).

Included among these investors were a number of grocers, butchers, joiners, etc, who were able to afford a larger deposit, and whose investment yielded a return of about 5½ per cent (ibid, 378, S10,926; Surveyors' Books 1851–2). Other investors borrowed to build on a larger scale. One such was Thomas Smith of Wakefield who in 1882 borrowed from the North Bierley Benefit Building Society to build sixty-six houses in Stanley (North Bierley Benefit Building Society Minute Book 1882, August 31). Another was John Crossland, who built twenty-two cottages in Holbeck, Leeds, in 1851, with a loan from the Leeds Permanent Building Society (Surveyors' Book 1851, 267). Such large-scale borrowing seems to have become increasingly common in the 1870s, the Chairman of the Leeds Permanent noting in 1884 that

> up to fourteen or fifteen years ago there was scarcely such a thing known as solicitors or capitalists borrowing money of the society. At the present time wealthy men in Leeds are taking advantage of it (Royal Commission on Housing 1884, 376, S10,869).

Employers, also, borrowed money from building societies for house-building projects. Edward Akroyd, for example, was helped by the Halifax Permanent Building Society to underwrite the cost of the houses at Akroydon, prior to repayment by the mortgagors (Bretton 1948, 79). The same society provided financial assistance for the Crossley's housing scheme at West Hill Park.

The most significant trend in the pattern of building society lending in the second half of the 19th century was the rapid increase in the size and number of loans made to speculative builders. In the Second Bradford Equitable Benefit Building Society at that time

> some advances were made to owners of single houses, but many more were made to builders and property investors (Lumb 1951, 20).

This society introduced a method of repayment in the late 1870s and early 1880s which helped speculators even more and so encouraged their borrowing. Instead of having to make regular payments, which would ultimately cover the cost of the capital plus interest, the borrower needed only to make payments to cover the interest. This was less costly for the speculator while he was building and, when he sold off his property, he repaid the borrowed capital in a lump sum. The advance and suspension policy, as it was called, was adopted by other building societies, including the Halifax Permanent, which, by the end of the century, made a large proportion of its loans to speculative builders by this method (Halifax Permanent General Ledger No 8 1877–1913, passim). Most of those who speculated in this way worked in the building trade, but there were others, such as 'travellers' and a draper, who were also involved (ibid). One society which tried to avoid lending to speculators was the Leeds Permanent –

> As to speculative builders, who of course swarm in every town, I do not know that we have half a dozen . . . in the Society . . . We do not advance them plenty of money (Royal Commission on Housing 1884, 377, S10,881).

Even this policy, however, was insufficient to prevent speculative builders from becoming the most important providers of workers' housing in Leeds by the late 19th century, many of them building society borrowers.

It was the building societies, therefore, which through their various systems of loans financed the later 19th-century boom in urban speculative house building as well as the provision of housing by individuals and smaller-scale investors. In Bradford, for example, the Second Bradford Equitable Benefit Building Society claimed to have

> helped finance the erection of many hundreds of the 'back-to-back' houses which formed the popular and acceptable method of housing . . . of these days (Lumb 1951, 8).

Population growth in Leeds increased the demand for housing there, too, and, like the Second Bradford Equitable, the Leeds Permanent Building Society claimed to have helped ease the pressure on accommodation:

Plate 102 (*above*).
Housing financed by
the Bradford Equitable
Building Society

Plate 103 (*left*).
Housing financed by
the Bradford Equitable
Building Society

Plate 104. Co-operative Society housing, Harriet Street, Brighouse

thousands of houses have been built and bought through this society by the working classes and by small capitalists (Royal Commission on Housing 1884, 371, S10,791).

The building societies played an important role in setting standards in house building, for in order to safeguard their interests they ensured that properties on which money was lent met certain minimum standards. The societies were mostly concerned with the structural quality of the houses built. In 1878 the Second Bradford Equitable's surveyor condemned 'the very jerry way in which Ayr and Laycock's property is being put up at Stanningley' (Lumb 1951, 16) and on one of the few occasions that a Leeds Permanent Surveyor condemned a cottage it was largely for structural faults:

The front and back walls are built of brick above the ground level – the end walls are of very rough stone parpoints [ie only one stone thick], and must have been done by a very indifferent workman. The slates are not collared at the gables. There are no spouts to the building and the house [living-room] floor is laid with very rough flags, the bedroom with old boards taken out of the other cottages. There are not any internal doors at present and the woodwork is not painted except the windows one coat. This property is so unsatisfactory that we cannot recommend the society to make *any grant* (Surveyors Book 1851–2, 284).

On the other hand, many of the cottages on which the Society gave loans seem to have been of a low standard in other respects, many of them back-to-backs. Although, by the 1870s and '80s, a substantial number of the houses built had two or even three bedrooms and a living-room, before that date the majority were far simpler. The cottages constructed by the Foxs in 1851 were typical of the dwellings built by borrowers at that time. Each of their cottages contained a cellar, a living-room and a single bedroom (Surveyors Book 1851–2, 202) and according to the surveyor who inspected them, they were 'plain and substantial' (*ibid*). No provision was made by the Foxs for conveniences or a water supply, items other builders also ignored. The majority of cottages built in the 1850s were generally provided with no source of water other than a rainwater tub, and privies, if they existed at all, were usually shared (Surveyor's Book 1851–2, *passim*). Some of the houses were built in cramped yards and there were even some loans for cellar dwellings (*ibid*, 251, 293). It is ironic that one pair of back-to-backs was considered to have been built too well:

> The roof is far too strong and expensive for buildings of this class and the furnishings generally are in our opinion too good for cottages producing the rental stated (Surveyors' Book 1851–2, 249).

In this case, presumably, the surveyor was concerned that the mortgagor had over-spent on his property.

As well as the building societies, a number of other associative bodies offered those individuals who could not, themselves, afford to build unaided a chance to acquire their own home. Foremost amongst these bodies were the county's numerous co-operative societies. The co-operative movement, from its origins in the 1820s, had, in practice, largely concerned itself with the retailing of provisions. By the 1860s, however, a number of societies were sufficiently prosperous to consider providing a wider range of benefits and services to their members, one such being the building of housing for their almost exclusively working-class memberships. As with other categories of house-builders, the scale of co-operative housing schemes became larger as the amount of capital available for investment increased. Brighouse Co-operative Society (founded in 1856), for example, began building cottages in 1865 on a small scale (Caldwell 1899, 192), but in 1869 formed a building committee to undertake larger projects. These included a development of twelve houses at Bailiff Bridge, built in 1877 in connection with a new store, and a crescent of sixteen houses erected in Brighouse, sold off to members by 1880 (Caldwell 1899, 207, 274). The society's largest undertaking was a development of forty-five houses in Rayner Road and Harriet Street, Brighouse (Pl 104). The houses which it provided were soundly built throughs, their good quality being largely attributable to the fact that the society was not principally motivated by the need or desire to make profits. In 1890 it proudly reported that,

> The society has not sought to make money on its cottage building schemes. The houses have been sold to members at the cost price, and the result is so gratifying that further schemes of this character might very well be developed (Caldwell 1899, 274).

Notes to Chapter 5
[1] As is shown by building societies' records of the loans they made, for example in the Halifax Building Society's General Ledgers.
[2] House plans submitted for approval by local government officials frequently bear an architect's name. See, for example, building plans submitted to the Bradford and Leeds corporations.

CHAPTER 6

IMPROVEMENT

There is a marked difference between the general standard of workers' housing built in the 1830s and 40s and that of the 1870s and 80s. Central to the improvement visible by the latter decades was a growing recognition of the desirability of improving the quality of this class of housing. Two of the most significant factors contributing to this improvement were the model dwellings movement and an increasing degree of governmental intervention.

The builders of model dwellings endeavoured to set an example to others by providing accommodation of a reasonable quality at an affordable rent, hoping to improve the quality of workers' housing by influencing those who built it (Gauldie 1974, 22; Pevsner 1943). The model builders were of great importance in that, although the quantity of housing they provided represented only a tiny proportion of the total built, they were very influential in the formulation of the concepts and building practices which were to form the basis of later government legislation. The government, too, became increasingly concerned over the question of the standards of workers' housing reflected by a growing amount of legislation on the subject which initially took the form of acts enabling local authorities to impose more stringent building regulations.

In the 1840s, both central and local government were being made aware of the inadequacies of much workers' housing. A report made by the Poor Law Board in 1842 found little to commend in the way in which the majority of the working population of England was housed at that time:

In the rural districts the worst of the new cottages are those erected on the borders of commons by the labourers themselves. In the manufacturing district, the tenements erected by building clubs and by speculative builders of the class of workmen, are frequently the subject of complaint as being the least substantial and the most destitute of proper accommodation. The only conspicuous instances of improved residences of the labouring classes found in the rural districts are those which have been erected by opulent and benevolent landlords for the accommodation of the labourers on their own estates; and in the manufacturing districts those erected by wealthy manufacturers for the accom-

modation of their own workforce (cited by Pevsner 1943, 121–2).[1]

The inadequacies of workers' accommodation were particularly apparent in those urban areas where unregulated housing developments of the late 18th and early 19th century had already degenerated into the slums which so alarmed both social and sanitary reformers. In those areas the problems of poor-quality housing were exacerbated by relatively high population densities. The Medical Officer of Health for Halifax reported in 1851 that:

The houses of the poor are closely built, badly ventilated and lighted and abounding in accumulations of offensive matter. The houses of the Irish are the worst in point of neglect and dirt (cited by Webster, 1978, 45).

Bradford also had its bad areas:

One general description will suffice for this street [Queen Street] and neighbourhood. It is a mess of filth – no drainage – the horse road unpaved, and nearly a foot deep in mud, together with stagnant water; houses generally crowded with men and women working together indiscriminately. The back parts of the streets on both sides, have filthy yards and cellars, in which the inmates are also crowded together to a great extent (Bradford Sanitary Committee 1845, 6).

Much the same conditions existed in Leeds in 1859:

The interspaces between the principal roads are occupied by dense and often complicated congeries of ill-kempt streets and courts which are in a very foul state (Medical Officer of Health, cited by Beresford 1971, 109);

and in 1860 George Godwin, editor of *The Builder*, noted that

The decent and comfortable houses of clerks and professional men bear a very slight proportion to the miles of squalid tenements in dirty badly drained streets, erected for artisans and millhands (*Builder* 1860, 809).

Contemporaries recognised that such overcrowding could nullify the effect of attempts to improve ventilation

Plate 105.
Miner's house,
Long Row, Nostell

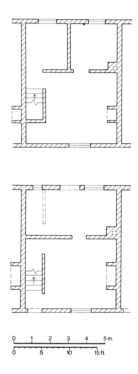

Fig 36.
No.17, Long Row, Nostell

and sanitation. They also realised that it could endanger health, The Halifax Medical Officer, for example, stating in 1851 that the overcrowded conditions of the poor were a fertile cause of disease (cited by Webster 1978, 45).

The problem of overcrowding was widespread in the poorer quarters of towns. In Halifax it was said that 'great numbers were found to herd together', in one instance the health committee inspectors finding eight beds in a two-roomed house (WYAS, Cal HXM: 419, 250). Some did not believe that overcrowding was a problem. One Halifax alderman, for example, felt it wrong to consider houses as overcrowded, despite the example of a family of twelve sleeping in three beds, or that of a widow with eight

children living in one cellar (Webster 1978, 46). Other people were more of the opinion of Robert Baker who, in 1842, expressed the view that

> It must be manifest that one sleeping room, though it may be quite sufficient for a young couple, must be very inadequate to a family of five persons, or more oftener eight (Baker 1842, 358).

Such problems were not exclusive to urban areas, many rural dwellings also being overcrowded. In the 1880s the average household living in the two and three-bedroomed cottages in Long Row, Nostell (37) (Pl 105, Fig 36) comprised ten or eleven members, over half the tenants

Plate 106 (*left*).
Urban housing,
East Leeds

Plate 107 (*right*).
Urban housing, East Leeds

taking in lodgers (Taylor 1978, 119). Some idea of the conditions in which the urban working-classes lived is given by the photographs taken in the late 19th century of earlier housing prior to its demolition (see Pls 106, 107).

IMPROVEMENT BY ENCOURAGEMENT

A growing awareness of the conditions in which large numbers of the working-classes lived stimulated various attempts to encourage improvement. One organisation which sought to do so was the Enclosures Commission, established in 1845, which was empowered to lend money for estate improvement and whose inspectors encouraged cottage building while imposing certain minimum standards. Their standards concerned such considerations as the provision of adequate sanitary arrangements and sufficient sleeping space and the use of properly seasoned timber and good-quality bricks (Gauldie 1974, 47). Further attempts were made to encourage estate owners to build cottages and to use improved plans by holding design competitions, publishing the winning plans in journals such as *The Builder* (Pl 108). West Yorkshire was not without its competitions for cottage designs, but the response to one held in 1860 by the Leeds Local Committee of the Royal Agricultural Society is perhaps significant. The competition had several different sections and for those concerned with agricultural cottages not one entry was submitted. Of the few plans which were received, all were of designs for the more profitable dense urban housing developments and all were considered to be substandard (*Builder* 1861, 182).

Some building societies tried to encourage model building. The Leeds Permanent made loans to the Cottage Society of Leeds and to the Society for the Erection of Improved Dwellings (Gauldie 1974, 202) while the Halifax Society helped to finance the model building schemes at Akroydon and West Hill Park, Halifax. The Halifax Society declared that it was not involved in the Akroydon scheme in order 'to provide "cheap" houses according to the popular acceptation of the word' but rather

> to erect, on the most advantageous terms, good substantial, healthy and comfortable homes, replete with every requisite convenience. *We have sought to improve the home of the working man and, by improving his home, to improve his health, his habits, his tastes and his character, and altogether to raise him in the social scale* (Alderson and Ogden 1921, 7).

Both Societies showed their concern to encourage the building of improved houses by preparing the plans of such houses which could be recommended to mortgagors. The cost of building the Leeds Permanent's houses ranged from £70 to £155, the cheapest dwellings being specifically aimed at their least-affluent mortgagors, whom they did not wish to be forgotten (Leeds Permanent Building Society 1948, 16). The Halifax Permanent produced plans of back-to-backs in blocks of four (Hobson 1953, 35). They also experimented with building tenemented blocks containing shops on the ground floor and different sized dwellings above (Gauldie 1974, 202–3). The idea behind this was that the more profitable shop rents would subsidize those from the one-roomed tenements in the block and enable low-income groups to occupy the latter while the block as a whole still yielded a return of 9 per cent (ibid, 203).

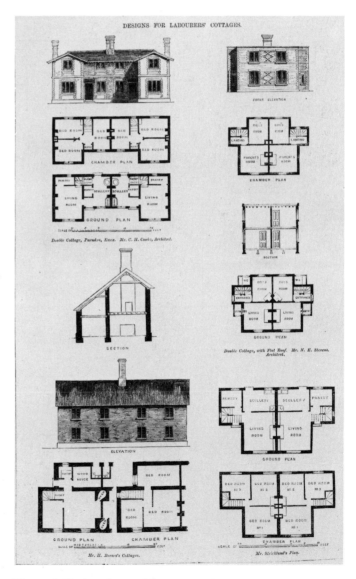

Plate 108. Designs for model cottages, 1860

IMPROVEMENT BY EXAMPLE

The realization in the mid-19th century of the inadequacies of a large proportion of workers' housing resulted in much public debate on the subject. *The Builder*, for example, was the forum for much discussion between architects, builders and others concerned with sanitation and public health, particularly in the 1860s. Some people became more practically involved, establishing model dwellings associations. One such society, established in Leeds in the 1850s, was the Model Cottage Society of Leeds, a non-profit-making organisation whose aim was to enable artisans to build themselves homes by acting as guarantor on loans from building societies. The Model Cottage Society hoped to ensure that houses of a good design and quality were built by providing improved plans for their beneficiaries to use and by regulating standards (Gauldie 1974, 202, 221; Tarn 1973, 14). Another model dwellings society operating in Leeds at this time was The Leeds Industrial Dwellings Company, which was responsible for building a block of small, galleried, tenements in Shannon Street in 1867 (*Builder* 1863, 193; Tarn 1973, 14). Other small model housing developments consisting of through houses were built in Leeds in Armley, Beeston, and Wortley (Hole 1866, 87, 212, 213; Pls 109, 110).

Despite their good intentions the work of these model dwellings associations was somewhat limited in effect. Their housing developments were small and did little to relieve the city's general housing problem. The associations also had problems in building improved housing cheaply enough for the intended occupants to be able to afford them. The Leeds Model Cottage Society, for example, originally intended its members to build through cottages with back yards and front gardens, but these proved to be too expensive and the Society's developments consisted, instead, of back-to-backs. These were, however, of the better sort, containing two bedrooms, a living-room, a scullery, a coal and keeping cellar and being equipped with water, gas, a set-pot and a sink. Even with the Society's help, however, this sort of property was beyond the means of many workers (Gauldie 1974, 202, 221; Tarn 1973, 14). One answer to this problem of providing cheap accommodation of a satisfactory standard was the building of tenements. As early as 1818, the architect John Loudon had designed this sort of building but it was not widely adopted, largely

Plate 109. Designs for model housing, Armley, Leeds

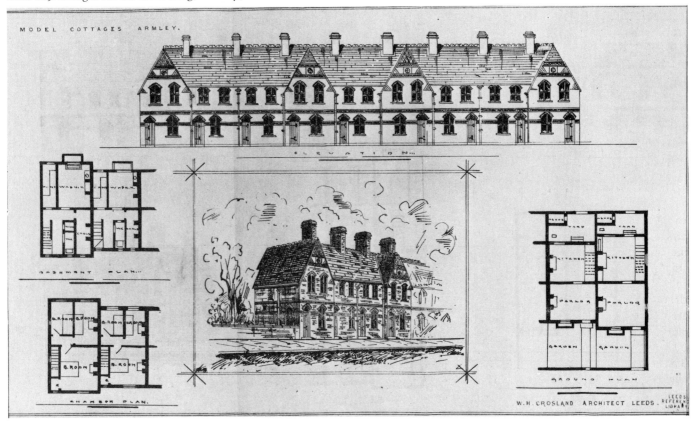

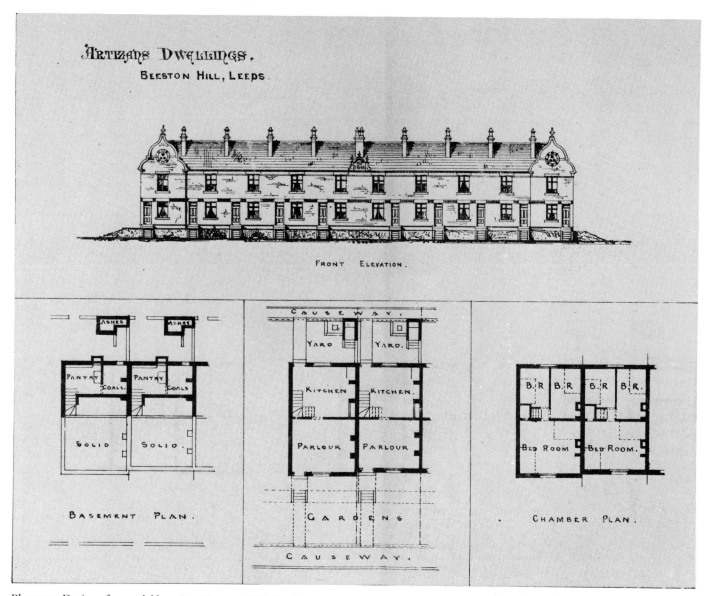

ARTIZANS DWELLINGS.
BEESTON HILL, LEEDS.

FRONT ELEVATION.

BASEMENT PLAN.

CAUSEWAY.

GARDENS

CAUSEWAY.

CHAMBER PLAN.

Plate 110. Designs for model housing, Beeston Hill, Leeds

because of the antipathy felt towards it by both builders and tenants alike (*ibid*, 128). In West Yorkshire a new departure came with the building by the Leeds Industrial Dwellings Company of tenemented blocks in Shannon Street. These dwellings were well appointed, each containing two or three bedrooms, a living-room, and a coal cupboard, with a shared water closet, access to a communal wash-house and arrangements for refuse collection in the basement (*Builder* 1867, 193).

The enthusiasm of model builders for tenements was not, however, shared by those for whom they were intended, despite their high quality in comparison with much contemporary workers' housing.

In order to keep costs down money was not usually spent on any architectural embellishments, which did nothing to help their popularity (Gauldie 1974, 223; Pevsner, 1943, 128). To maintain standards within the blocks, moreover, conditions were generally imposed on the tenants, and these, too, were resented (ibid). It was not only prospective tenants who disliked the tenement system: it seems to have been regarded as a matter for congratulation to the local Medical Officer of Health in 1884 that Leeds was 'remarkably free' of tenements (Parliamentary Papers 1885, Vol 2; Royal Commission on Housing 1884, 326, S9783). For the builder, also, tenements were not an attractive proposition. In 1865 it was estimated that such dwellings rarely produced a dividend larger than 5 per cent, an uncompetitive rate, and tenements were, moreover, a greater risk and more troublesome to the builder than were superior houses (Pevsner 1943, 121, 128). Since most builders were governed more by economic factors than by considerations of design and the standard of facilities, it is not surprising that the example set by the model dwellings associations had only a limited following.

Amongst those who did follow their lead and who contributed to the movement were a number of employers. In some cases an employer was motivated by a sense of responsibility for his workers' welfare. Edward Akroyd, for example, stated that he had built the houses at Copley

> not merely for the purpose of aggregating a sufficient number of operatives for the supply of labour, but also with an eye to the improvement of their social condition, by fitting up their houses with every requisite comfort and convenience (cited by Bretton 1948, 75).

Where employers did feel responsible for their work forces the provision of housing of good quality was a very tangible way of discharging that duty. Titus Salt at Saltaire, Edward Akroyd at Akroydon and the Crossleys at West Hill Park, were all influenced by enlightened contemporary opinion on housing standards. Other employers were also affected by such opinions, some building to high standards even if not attempting to provide model housing. Such was the case at Dewsbury Mills, St Mary's Court, Wilshaw, Calmlands, Meltham, and in other employers' housing developments. As was the case with model dwelling associations, however, the immediate effect of such builders was limited. Although they were concerned to prove to others that well-built housing could bring a reasonable return, their developments were not profitable enough to win over a significant number of fellow manufacturers. At Akroydon there was a 6 per cent return on the houses, which Akroyd believed 'gave no reason to complain' (Bretton 1948, 81), but his earlier venture at Copley had yielded only 4½ per cent interest on the outlay and even 6 per cent compared unfavourably with the return to be made on poorer-quality housing.[2] Builders of improved dwellings were also faced with the difficulty of finding tenants prepared to pay the higher rents carried by this better-quality housing, a not insignificant factor which Akroyd, for one, identified as part of the problem:

> at present the working classes are so little accustomed to a really good house, of a pleasing elevation, and fitted up with every convenience, that they are unwilling to pay the increased cost (cited by Bretton 1948, 81).

Such reluctance would have done little to encourage the majority of builders to follow the standards of those who provided model accommodation.

IMPROVEMENT BY ENFORCEMENT

In the second half of the 19th century a number of acts were passed by parliament in an attempt to improve the standard of workers' housing. Behind this legislation lay feelings of social responsibility and, perhaps, philanthropy, but there was also a large element of self-interest. Although cholera and other diseases were most frequently associated with the worst urban housing, once an epidemic had started it was no respecter of wealth or status. It was stated in the preamble to the Artisans' and Labourers' Dwellings Improvement Act of 1875 that the insanitary and unhealthy conditions of large numbers of houses in the towns generated death and ill-health 'not only in the courts and alleys but also in other parts of such cities and boroughs' (cited by Wilson 1971, 203). Particularly virulent outbreaks in the mid-19th century of cholera and other diseases did much to convince government of the necessity of sanitary reforms. Linked with this task was a recognised need to improve the sanitation, ventilation and structural quality of much workers' housing.[3]

Starting with the Towns Improvement Clauses Act 1847, a series of permissive acts was passed empowering the local authorities to make bye-laws on an increasing number of issues. These were concerned primarily with urban health and safety and related to sanitation, the healthiness of houses, their structural stability and their inflammability (Public General Statutes 1847, 256–8, 380–424; 1867–8 950; 1875, 256–8; Royal Commission on Housing 1884, Vol II, 21, 22). Although each urban authority formulated its own bye-laws, these were, in fact, almost identical, for not only did the authorities follow the content and often the wording of national legislation, but they generally had the same problems to cope with and their primary concerns were similar. The bye-laws were not, however, particularly innovative. Considering the earlier, better-built workers' housing and that provided by model builders, it is true to say that, rather than introducing novel concepts, bye-laws codified the best of existing building practices, many of which had been put into effect by those concerned to provide good-quality housing. It was, therefore, in the role of initiators of higher building standards and practices that the model builders were most significant. In many cases bye-laws followed their lead so that, either indirectly or directly, both were agents in the general improvement of housing standards which occurred in the second half of the 19th century. (For a recent discussion of building bye-laws see Gaskell 1983.)

THE PROCESS OF IMPROVEMENT

By the mid-19th century the requirements of model builders, according to John Loudon, were that houses should be 'warm, dry, light, well-ventilated and convenient' (Loudon 1840, 8). In addition there should be 'an ample supply of good water' and 'the number and area of its apartments must be in proportion to the number of occupants, and a due provision made for a well-ordered family life' (*Builder* 1860, 476). Much of what the model builders desired was dictated by their concern that housing should be healthy, in order to ensure both the physical and moral well-being of their occupants.

From the point of view of providing healthy housing, good drainage and sewerage were, in the words of one contemporary, 'an absolute necessity' (*Builder* 1860, 431). The social reformer James Hole was a local proponent of healthy housing, observing that good drainage had 'in numerous instances led to an immediate and very large diminution of the rate of mortality' (Hole 1866, 10). At Akroydon (102) the houses were 'thoroughly drained with sanitary tubes' approved of by the editor of *The Builder* (*Builder* 1863, 110). The issue of drainage and sewerage featured prominently in local authority bye-laws, the problems caused by the inadequacies of such facilities being exacerbated in urban environment. In Leeds in 1866, for example, Hole condemned the fact that, 'there are many miles of houses, yards, and streets *unconnected with the main drainage*' (*Builder* 1860, 809). It was at about this time that bye-laws began to require houses to be serviced by well-constructed, ventilated drains, made of impermeable materials in order to prevent seepage. Bye-laws concerning street drainage also affected houses, requiring properties to have gutters, drainpipes and underground drains to carry off surface water and rain (Bradford 1897, 1; Halifax 1850, 15; Leeds 1842, 81). Such provisions, as well as keeping the streets drier and so more healthy, helped alleviate one cause of dampness in house walls. Similar considerations of health underlay the bye-laws which forbade the building of houses on land previously used for dumping refuse until certain remedial action had been taken (bye-law of 1889 cited in Bradford 1897, 21; Leeds 1878, 5) and which banned the practice of keeping pigs in living-accommodation (Leeds 1838, 17; Leeds 1842, 96; Halifax 1850, 14).

The provision of an adequate number of privies and night soil pits, together with the removal of filth and manure collected in them, was another aspect of sanitation which caused concern to contemporaries. The ideal of model builders was that each house should have its own privy, set in individual, high-walled yards to ensure privacy (Hole 1866, 5). This ideal was attained at Akroydon (102), Calmlands, Meltham (91), Saltaire (114) and West Hill Park

(42), but more frequently the privies were shared. The cost of water closets tended to prohibit their use in workers' housing at this time. It was originally intended to provide them at Akroydon, but the plan was dropped in view of the high charge the Corporation would have made for supplying them with water (Linstrum and Powell 1977, 12). Bye-laws gradually imposed more stringent requirements as to privy and ash-pit provision, but it was a long time before the deficiency was remedied. In 1861 certain areas of Halifax were still badly served in this respect, 13 per cent of the cottages in the North Ward having no access at all to a privy or ash-pit and one group of fifty dwellings sharing only three privies and two ash-pits between them (WYAS, Cal. HXM 420, 240). The situation was no better in Leeds, where Hole exclaimed in 1860:

> One privy to *four* cottages has been settled to be the legitimate allowance but this liberality of supply has been by no means universally attained. A favourite plan, and almost inevitable on the back-to-back system of building, is to plant the privies for a number of houses in the centre of a row, with a sleeping chamber over! (*Builder* 1860, 809).

The latter practice, at least, was prohibited in 1866 when it was decreed that no rooms built over such conveniences should be used for habitation (Leeds 1901, 77, 274, 276). This bye-law would have put an effective end to cottages being built like those in St John's Court, Leeds (70), where the end dwelling had an extra bedroom situated above the privies (see Pl 53, Fig 27). By the 1870s local authorities generally required a privy to be provided for every dwelling (although in Leeds the requirement was as little as one privy to every four (Hole 1866)), specifications being made as to their size, the removal of manure and refuse from them (Idle 1864, 23), and their distance away from dwellings.

To increase the effects of improved sanitation and to ensure cleanliness it was believed that an adequate water supply was necessary. In 1840 Loudon felt it essential that 'every cottager should be perfectly independent in respect of water' (Loudon 1840, 9). Hole echoed this view in 1866, believing that water should be piped to every house. Again, model builders led the way on this issue, water being piped to the houses at Copley, Saltaire, Akroydon, West Hill Park and Robinwood Terrace, Todmorden. Local authorities were given the right to demand that dwellings be provided with a water supply. In 1857 in Halifax, for example, the owner of certain cottages at Old Bank was ordered to connect them with water-pipes (WYAS Cal, HXM 157, 354). In Bradford the Corporation went so far as to provide piped water, paid for by the rates (Thompson 1982, 149). Many houses, however, still went without. As late as 1902 it

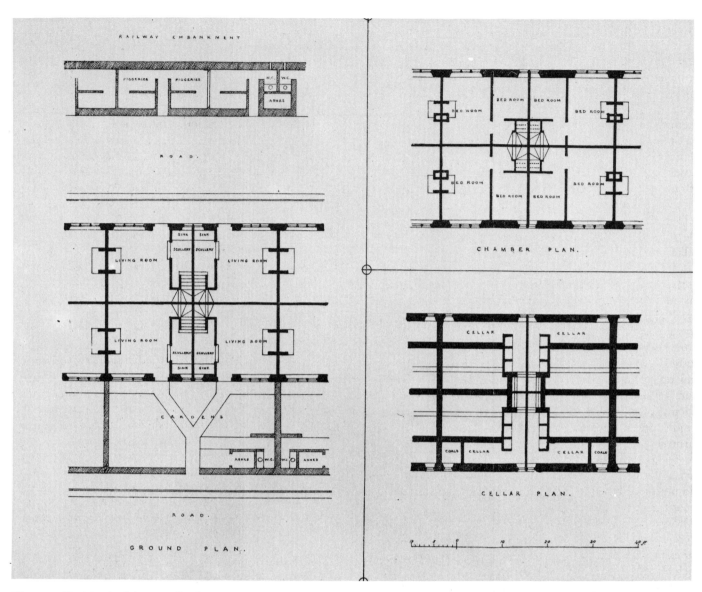

Plate 111. Back-to-back houses, Copley

was reported of Pontefract that 'a very large number of the working class houses have no water provided inside them', relying instead on standpipes (JGLC County Medical Officer 1903, 347). Local authorities were also empowered to demand the provision of sinks and drains, a right assumed by the Bradford Corporation in 1881 (Bradford 1897, 22). Model builders, also, favoured the inclusion in houses of sinks and set-pots (*Builder* 1860, 476). The twelve houses in St Mary's Court, Wilshaw (92), had to share a single water pump, but each had its own sink and set-pot for boiling washing. By the time these houses were built, in 1873, the latter features were not confined to model housing, being provided in most new houses (WYAS, Bradford Building Plans 1873). Model builders, however, on occasion provided better facilities than that which even housing reformers believed to be desirable. At Saltaire Titus Salt went so far as to provide communal wash-houses with drying-rooms and, in addition, public baths to encourage personal cleanliness (Dewhirst 1960–1, 141).

Good ventilation was believed to be another requisite to ensure the healthiness of dwellings and to achieve this, model builders thought that a through draught of air was essential.[4] The 'want of ventilation' and stuffiness of urban dwellings were frequently condemned as contributing to their unhealthiness (WYAS Cal, HXM 156, 250). Sanitary reformers were opposed to cellar dwellings and back-to-back houses because they did not allow the necessary 'free ventilation of pure air' (Builder 1860, 476). Model builders themselves, therefore, never provided cellar-dwelling accommodation, but many such existed in the towns. In Bradford cellar dwellings were still in 1845 'the chief residences of the lower grades of the working classes' (Bradford Sanitary Committee 1845, 14), while in Leeds they formed 3 per cent of all accommodation. Many of these cellars were inadequate as dwellings. After an inspection in 1857, Halifax Corporation found that 85 per cent of the 311 cellar dwellings in the town were defective either in having too low ceilings, insufficient window area or not enough open areas adjoining (WYAS Cal, HXM 157). In some instances ordinary cellars, as opposed to purpose-built cellar dwellings, were used as accommodation. In Bradford there was a case of a coal cellar only 3 ft (0.915m) wide slept in by three adults (Bradford Sanitary Committee 1845, 3). Local authorities gradually moved towards a ban on the building and occupation of cellar dwellings, against much opposition. In Halifax owners ordered to improve such dwellings acted dilatorily (WYAS Cal, HXM 158, 359, 391), while in Bradford the Property Owners' Protection Society was formed to resist the Corporation's attempts to close cellar dwellings. Landlords and tenants there also colluded to defeat the bye-law banning them, owners saying that they did not receive rent on the cellars as separate properties and tenants that the cellar dwellings were part of a shared house (Thompson 1980, 162; Wright 1982, 48). Local authorities were more successful in imposing certain improvements, for example in Leeds, where from 1842 it was required that such dwellings be provided with a window, a fireplace and an area at least 3 ft (0.915m) wide (Leeds 1901, 75). Eventually the authorities succeeded in passing bye-laws prohibiting the building of more cellar dwellings and closing defective ones. Such legislation came into effect in Halifax in 1869 when 'a very large number' of cellar dwellings were given notice to be cleansed and ventilated 'to the satisfaction of the Sanitary Inspector' (WYAS Cal HXM 157, 491). In Bradford no new ones were built after 1854 (Wright 1982, 147–8) and by 1860 James Hole was able to report that 'the Corporation has closed most of the cellar dwellings'. However, pressure on housing in the 1860s led to the reoccupation of some of the condemned cellars (Wright 1982, 147–8).

In Leeds such dwellings continued to be occupied into the late 19th century. These would have been the better-quality ones, since the worst dwellings had been removed by the Corporation's closure policy:

Since I have been Medical Officer of Health I have closed batch after batch of cellars; we close them and do not allow them to be built in the new artisans' houses (Royal Commission on Housing 1884, 527, S9843).

On the issue of cellar dwellings housing reformers had a large body of public opinion behind them. The subject of back-to-back housing, which many reformers also wished to have prohibited, was a far more contentious issue and one on which even those concerned for the best interests of the occupants of such houses could not agree. The arguments against back-to-back were summed up in 1871 by one sanitary reformer after a visit to Leeds:

The plan is necessarily unwholesome from the absence of any through ventilation of the several cottages; and it renders impossible the decent and proper provision of a privy or water-closet attached to each house (cited in West Yorkshire forthcoming).

Other people, however, were of the opinion voiced by the Leeds Town Clerk in 1841 that to ban back-to-backs would drive the working classes into lodgings, since they could not, or would not, afford higher rents (Burnett 1978, 76). The back-to-back house, moreover, was often preferred to others by the inhabitants, the Leeds Medical Officer of Health still finding in 1884 that,

the working people of Leeds would rather have back-to-backs than houses open at the back which I myself suggested some four or five years ago, and which I thought was an improvement (Royal Commission on Housing 1884, 327, S9825).

Model builders, being concerned to provide the healthiest dwellings possible, were influenced against the back-to-back. The houses at Akroydon and Saltaire were all built as throughs, while the competition for the design of houses at West Hill Park specifically stipulated, 'none of the houses to be "back-to-back" ' (West Hill Park Competition 1863). A decade earlier the houses at Copley had been built to that plan (Pl 111), on which grounds they were criticized:

this is the greatest social and sanitary drawback to the otherwise successful character of the dwellings. There can be no apology for back-to-back houses; and though it is one of the common features of the country in this neighbourhood, we believe strongly efforts are now being made to put a stop to the practice (Builder 1863, 109).

It is significant that when a further twenty-four cottages were built, c. 1865, they were built in two rows as throughs,

Plate 112.
Through houses, Copley

a narrow alley separating the two terraces (Pl 112). Apart from this difference the through cottages were the same in size and plan as the earlier back-to-backs. It may be that their design was influenced by contemporary disapproval of the back-to-back plan but, if the idea had been to give the cottages the benefit of through ventilation, the plan was not entirely satisfactory, the back door being situated under the stairs and separated from the living-room by a second door. Nor was use made of the free-standing rear wall to provide windows which would have facilitated a through draught. Other builders made little or no concession to the idea of throughs being preferable to back-to-backs. At West Vale, Dewsbury (34) (Cook, Hague and Wormald's Mill-housing), and Derby Terrace, Marsden (85), the back-to-back plan was used as late as 1873 and 1879 respectively, although the cottages were of a high standard in other particulars.

Local opposition hampered the process of prohibitive legislation. In Bradford, where approximately 76 per cent of the houses in the 1850s were back-to-backs, a bye-law of 1860 effectively banned such dwellings by requiring a certain amount of open space around individual houses. The strength of opposition to this bye-law was such, however, that, when it was coupled with increasing population pressure on existing housing, the corporation had to retract, modifying the bye-law a few years later (Hole 1866, 38 note; Wright 1982, 148; Reynolds 1983, 245). The result of

compromise, in Bradford and elsewhere, was that, although back-to-backs continued to be built, they were a great improvement on earlier, similar, dwellings. Compliance with local authority regulations produced a standard type of dwelling, many of its features the result of meeting the bye-law requirements. In Bradford, for example, back-to-backs built in the 1870s had to have a minimum of one back yard to every four houses. This yard had to extend the full width of the houses it served, measure a minimum of 12 feet (3.657 m) in every direction, be enclosed by a wall at least 4 feet (1.22 m) tall to ensure privacy and contain at least one ash-pit and a privy for each house. Between every two pairs of houses there was to be a passage giving access to the rear area, at least one storey high and 6 feet 6 inches (1.982 m) wide. Each house was to have a door or window onto this passage, thus ensuring both a more satisfactory means of ventilation and a more private means of access to the back yard for occupants of the front houses (which were the ones supplied with the side doors) (Bradford 1870, 7–9) (see Southampton St Fig 52). In 1881 further legislation was passed concerned with the structure of the passages to the back yards, requiring a minimum wall thickness of 9 inches (29 mm) and making specifications about the timbers used to bridge the passage and carry the upper storey of the dwellings above it (Bradford 1897, 2). In 1875 a typical Bradford 'bye-law back-to-back' as they have been called, contained a coal and keeping cellar, a living-room on the ground floor, and two bedrooms above. It was provided with an ash-pit and 'suitable conveniences' and might have a small front garden (Lumb 1951, facing 22). A superior type of back-to-back had a side-scullery on the ground floor and a third, attic, bedroom (Pl 127, Fig 53). After 1870 no new plans for back-to-backs were approved by Bradford Corporation although, since plans which had previously received approval could still be built, their construction continued for some time (Bradford Building Regulations 1910, 54). In Leeds the Corporation did not act to prevent approval of back-to-back plans until 1909, when required to do so by national legislation. It was not until 1937, however, that the last back-to-backs were built, their plans having been approved prior to that legislation (Beresford 1971, 117).

The concern to ensure good ventilation, evident in the opposition to both cellar dwellings and back-to-backs, affected attitudes not only towards house types in general but also to more detailed aspects of house design. It was believed, for example, that tall ceilings were desirable in order that air could circulate freely within rooms. Recognizing the validity of this argument municipal legislators passed bye-laws which imposed minimum ceiling heights. However, although this would allow air to circulate within rooms this was of little benefit unless the air was fresh. To ensure that it was, model builders equipped their houses with large windows. These were generally designed as sashes, with at least one half openable (*Builder* 1860, 476). The windows in the cottages at West Vale, Dewsbury (34), and Calmlands, Meltham (91), were even larger than usual (Pls 113, 114).

Plate 113 (*above*).
Mill housing, West Vale, Dewsbury

Plate 114 (*right*).
Mill housing, Royd Edge, Meltham

Air bricks, also, were used to ventilate rooms. In towns, bye-laws were passed in an attempt to improve ventilation in the houses of the poor, where, it was felt,

> ventilation is neither understood nor regarded – windows are generally fixed in their sashes or if they open at all are so small as to be almost useless for admitting light or air. Many of the rooms have no fireplace and in those that have the chimney is often carefully closed (cited by Webster 1978, 45).

In the 1860s bye-laws required there to be at least one window in each habitable room, half of it openable, and the whole in area comprising one-tenth of the floor area of the room.

The provision of large windows, as well as letting in fresh air, fulfilled another contemporary requirement, namely that dwellings be well lit (*Builder* 1860, 476). In his competition design for West Hill Park, G W Stevenson's houses had large windows for the avowed purpose of 'affording abundant light and air' (West Hill Park Competition 1863). Fanlights above front and back doors also increased the light inside a passage or room, becoming a common feature in houses from the mid-19th century. They were used at West Vale (34), Calmlands (71) and West Hill Park (42). The introduction of gas lighting presented further possibilities for providing well-lit dwellings, but, although it was used at Akroydon and in the later cottages at Copley, the expense entailed in its provision was generally prohibitive. The use of features such as fanlights and stair windows, when compared to the scanty provision in earlier (and many contemporary) houses, show the extent to which considerations of internal convenience advanced as a design concept in the mid-19th century, even in houses built for working people.

Employers who built housing of a good standard were no doubt influenced, not only by the arguments of sanitary reformers, but also by the consideration that soundly built cottages would last longer and need less maintenance than would shoddily built dwellings. Good-quality materials were used and structural considerations were also taken into account. At West Vale (34) and St Mary's Court (55), for example, the large, ground-floor windows were built with relieving arches above them to prevent the lintels sagging under the pressure of the wall and roof. Similarly, in their plans for houses at West Hill Park, the architects, Paul and Aycliffe, positioned first-floor partitions above those on the ground floor wherever possible, in order to relieve the upper floor structure (West Hill Park Competition 1863).

By the mid-19th century the benefits of other structural features had also been recognised. Cavity walls were used 'with a view to warmth and dryness' (*Builder* 1860, 431), as at West Hill Park (West Hill Park Competition 1863).

Damp-proof courses were sometimes used but did not become a standard feature until later in the century. Additional comfort was given to dwellings by plastering the walls (*Builder* 1860, 431), as was done at Akroydon (*Builder* 1863, 110), and by providing a sufficient number of fireplaces with flues designed to prevent their smoking (*Builder* 1860, 476).

Local authorities also became interested in the quality of construction of houses. The reasons for their involvement were, however, rather different from those of model builders, the principal concerns within towns being to ensure the structural stability and therefore the safety of properties and to reduce their inflammability. The former consideration resulted in bye-laws specifying minimum wall thicknesses (generally 9 inches (229 mm) if built of brick, or 12 inches (305 mm) if of stone), their proper bonding and the width of cavities in hollow walls.[5] Concern for fire-prevention led to stipulations that walls should be plastered, chimneys and flues should be soundly built, of good materials and of a design to prevent smoking, that roofs, chimneys and flues should be built of incombustible materials, that hearthstones should be provided in front of fireplaces, that woodwork should not be placed too near the latter and that well pointed party walls should extend from the foundations to the upper side of the ceiling joists.[6]

In order to ensure that houses were built according to bye-law regulations, local authorities required building plans to be submitted for approval (Bradford 1865, 10; Halifax 1869, 12) and subsequently inspected the houses which were constructed. Plans which did not meet requirements were rejected (Bradford Building Plans) and action was taken against builders who did not submit plans before construction or deviated from the plans approved (WYAS Cal. HXM 158, 509, 510).

Housing was also affected by certain environmental considerations which model-builders and urban legislators believed to be important. Housing reformers realized that the effectiveness of provisions for ventilation were helped or hindered by the amount of open space immediately surrounding a house. Wide streets were thought to be essential if satisfactory ventilation was to be ensured. Hole believed a minimum width of 60 feet (18.29 m) to be necessary (Hole 1866, 33), but this was never practicable. At Akroydon, where the streets were said to be 'of good width so as to afford ample space for ventilation' (cited by Bretton 1948, 81) the front streets were 35 feet (10.67m) wide and the back streets 20 feet (60.10m) (excluding front gardens and back yards). These measurements were as great as any adopted elsewhere and similar to those required by urban legislators.[7] Bye-laws concerned with street widths began to be made in the 1840s, requiring progressively wider and more spacious streets. Free circulation of air was particularly

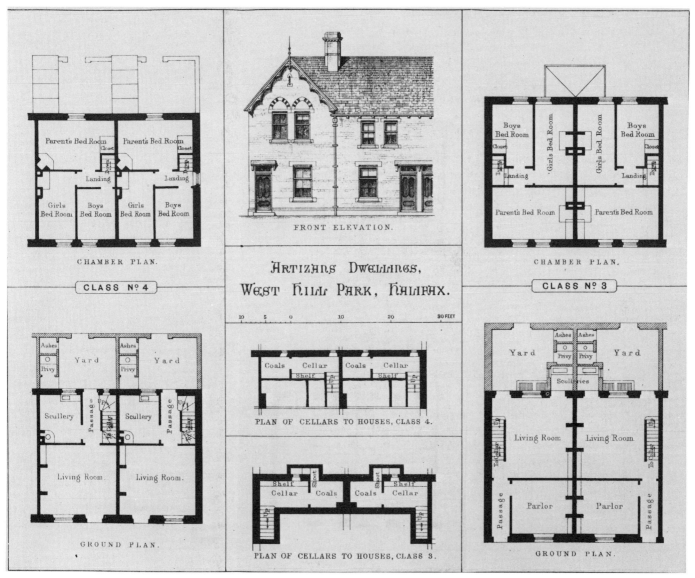

Plate 115. Architects' plans for housing at West Hill Park, Halifax

restricted in the narrow, crowded, urban courts. Local authorities tried to improve the situation by making requirements as to the width of courts and the means of access to them (Halifax 1869, 6). The first attempt made in Leeds, in 1842, was not, however, entirely successful, being 'found insufficient for remedying the evils' of such courts (Leeds 1870, 11). Further legislation was passed reiterating earlier stipulations, and eventually forbidding the building of houses in courts altogether (Leeds 1878, 25; Leeds 1901, 71, 273).

The desire of model builders to improve the quality of life of the occupants of their houses led them to consider further aspects of house design. Concern for the inhabitants' moral welfare resulted in an emphasis on the necessity of providing enough bedrooms for male and female children to sleep in different rooms. George Godwin, editor of *The Builder*, proclaimed in 1860 that,

> there should always be three [bedrooms]; so that the male and female children may be separated. Cottages for families with only two bedrooms lead to an incredible amount of vice (*Builder* 1860, 126).

Similar sentiments were expressed by other contemporaries (Bradford Sanitary Commitee 1845 passim) and Godwin soundly criticized houses at Akroydon which were provided with only two bedrooms. (*Builder* 1863, 110). At West Hill Park the rules of the competition for designing the houses specified that all grades should have three bedrooms (Pl 115). This number was provided in the houses at

Calmlands, Meltham (91), Robinwood Terrace, Todmorden (139) and in the larger houses at Saltaire; while at St Mary's Court, Wilshaw (92) a third bedroom was provided by building an attic room over part of the first floor (Fig 37). Godwin suggested that the deficiency at Akroydon be remedied by dividing the largest bedroom into two with a partition (*Builder* 1863, 110) but to have followed this suggestion, either at Akroydon and elsewhere, would have made the rooms ridiculously small (*Builder* 1860, 142). Since a bed could be put in the living-room adequate segregation could be achieved with only two bedrooms and this, therefore, was the practical minimum number. An interesting compromise was made in the back-to-backs in Derby Terrace, Marsden (85) (Pl 116, Fig 38) where each dwelling was provided with two bedrooms on the first floor. There was room for only one attic room above and, this being allocated to the front dwelling, the result was a mixture of two and three-bedroomed houses. Not all well-built housing was provided with two bedrooms. At Copley many of the cottages had only one bedroom, a reflection of the fact that the village was built before the crystallization of many of the ideas on model housing (Webster 1978, 47).

The idea of the value of privacy was filtering down to builders of workers' housing by the mid-19th century. In their houses at West Hill Park Paull and Aycliffe departed from the traditional design of the front door opening directly into the living-room. Instead, it opened into an entrance passage off which ran the stairs, 'by which means', they asserted, 'the privacy of the lower rooms is thus secured, which at times of medical or other visits to the bedroom, will be a great convenience' (West Hill Park Competition 1863).

This design, in addition, protected the living-room from a direct draught when the front door was opened. Paull and Aycliffe also stressed that they had separated the front and back doors as widely as possible from those of the adjoining houses

> thus preventing, as far as possible, the evils attendant upon close proximity, which are too well known to need further comment (West Hill Park Competition 1863).

Some model builders were concerned to provide sufficient storage space. A small upstairs room, or closet, for clothes were considered

> a most desirable thing in a cottage: as wardrobes, presses, etc, do not form part of a poor man's furniture, consequently the bedrooms are always in an untidy and fluttered state, unless a closet be provided (*Builder* 1861, 536).

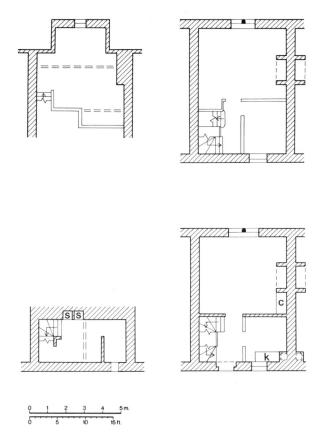

Fig 37. St. Mary's Court, Wilshaw

Such closets were provided at Akroydon in the houses in Ripon Terrace, and at Calmlands. More common were the large wall-cupboards which became a standard feature in cottages from the mid-19th century. Cellars were another common feature from this time, although they were omitted at West Hill Park to prevent their being misused as wash-rooms (West Hill Park Competition 1863). There were some complaints that occupants were misusing the accommodation with which they were provided. At Akroydon Godwin criticized the fact that the larger houses had both a kitchen and a living room because families used the larger room as a best Sunday parlour, crowding into the kitchen for everyday purposes (*Builder* 1863, 110). This was a problem which arose, however, only in larger houses, since the majority of workers' houses were provided with only a living-room and a scullery and often without the latter, this being the case at West Vale (34) and Holme Villas, Lingards Wood (75). Another feature that appeared first of all in larger houses and was assimilated only gradually into smaller ones was the provision of fireplaces in at least two bedrooms (*Builder* 1860, 476). In the houses in

Plate 116. Derby Terrace, Marsden

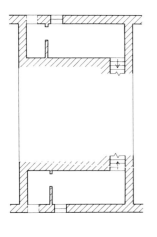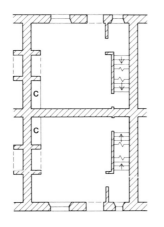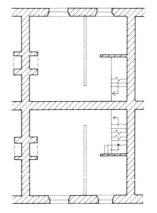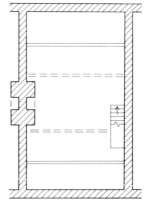

0 1 2 3 4 5m.

0 5 10 15ft.

Fig 38. Derby Terrace, Marsden

Plate 117. Robinwood Terrace, Todmorden

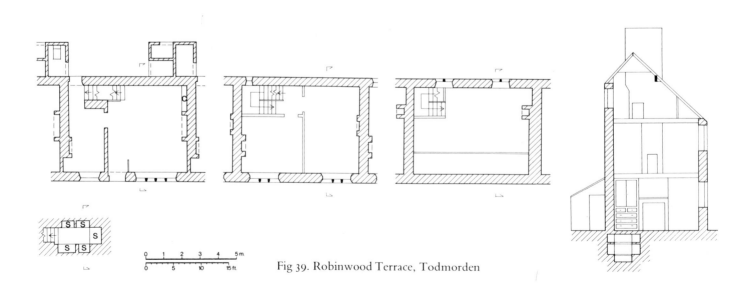

Fig 39. Robinwood Terrace, Todmorden

Plate 118. Akroydon Co-operative Store (1861)

Robinwood Terrace, Todmorden (139) this minimum was exceeded, all three bedrooms being heated (Pl 117, Fig 39).

The concern of model builders for their tenants' welfare was expressed not only in the standard of the accommodation they built, but also in other provisions which they made. One of Titus Salt's reasons for building his model village in what was, at that time, a rural location was that it would remove his employees to a healthy atmosphere. Although the houses and mill comprised a fairly dense development they were within easy reach of the countryside. Salt provided, moreover, a park on the river bank, with cricket and croquet grounds and a bowling green (Dewhirst 1961, 141). Gardening was considered a healthy recreation, many employers either supplying houses with a garden or offering tenants the opportunity to take up an allotment. At Copley a horticultural society was established to encourage this pursuit and gardening competitions run

(Bretton 1948, 74–75), while at West Hill Park Paull and Aycliffe even proposed putting earth on the privy roofs to be used as flower beds (West Hill Park Competition 1863). Some of the larger employers, including Akroyd, the Crossleys, Fieldens and Salt, provided a wide range of other communal facilities, including schools, reading rooms, places of worship and almshouses. Penny Banks and co-operative shops were encouraged at Akroydon (Pl 118) and Copley, while, at the latter a dining shed was provided. Even where employers were less concerned to provide model communities they recognized the benefits of educational and other amenities, schools being built near Holme Villas, Lingards Wood (75) and Derby Terrace, Marsden (85).

Textile employers were not alone in providing institutes of this kind. Colliery companies responsible for large-scale housing developments also provided schools, reading

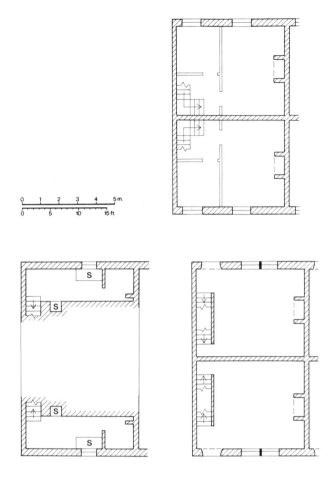

rooms, recreation grounds, places of worship (University of Leeds MS 160, 6, 7, 72; Goodchild 1976, 8, 11, 21–28; Goodchild 1977, 11, 13; Lewis 1971, 37; Taylor 1978, 6) and, at Low Moor, free medical attention for employees and their families (Dodsworth 1971, 142). Colliery company involvement was at its greatest at Sharlston where, apart from providing the chapel and school, the company encouraged various clubs, founded a Penny Bank, a literary institute with a reading room, library and coffee room, and established a co-operative store. That company involvement at Sharlston was more like that of the textile employers' approach than that of other colliery companies' is probably due to the fact that the New Sharlston Colliery Company was financially supported by the Crossley family, builders of West Hill Park. Francis Crossley even went so far as to buy out a Sharlston worker's beer shop, being concerned to keep the village alcohol-free (Goodchild 1976, 22–23).

When building houses, some employers provided a variety of sizes or types. In 1866 Hole recommended that this should be done in order to cater for workers with differing wage rates (Hole 1866, 39). Hole, presumably, believed that all grades of house should be throughs, but in practice this was not always the case. At Long Row, New Sharlston (110) the cheapest cottages, making up nearly half the row, were back-to-backs (Goodchild 1976, 20). Similarly, at West Vale (34) the lower-grade houses were back-to-backs (Fig 40). Elsewhere differentiation was made even when all the houses were throughs. At Nostell there was a mixture of two and three-bedroomed colliers' cottages in Long Row (37) while officials lived in a different terrace nearer the workings (Taylor 1978, 119). In Outwood, Stanley, another terrace occupied by colliery foremen still retains its name of Deputy Row; within it there were two grades of house, varying slightly in size (Pl 119; Fig 41). Different grades of housing were generally separated, at West Hill Park the architects endeavouring 'to limit the look-out from each class of house, to cottages of a similar and not inferior character' (West Hill Park Competition 1863). A similar concern was shown at West Vale, Dewsbury, where, although the back-to-backs and slightly larger throughs were situated together, a terrace of superior houses for managers was separated from the smaller dwellings by a canal cutting. Both Salt and Akroyd intermingled housing of different grades at Saltaire and Akroydon (but not at Copley). Akroyd's stated aim in so doing was to benefit poorer tenants by bringing them into contact with those who were more affluent (*Builder* 1863, 110). Naturally this sort of paternalism was not always appreciated and Akroyd's housing venture was treated by some suspicion (Facer and Gasse 1980, 19).

The effect of model builders in influencing contemporary opinion on housing standards and of the local authorities in

Fig 40. Back-to-backs, West Vale, Dewsbury

legislating on such issues was to improve the standard of a large proportion of workers' housing. Had prospective occupants been unable or unwilling to pay the increased cost of this housing, however, there would have been less chance of improvement.[8] As it was, improvement occurred not only in urban and model housing, but on a wider front. These improvements are evident as far down the housing scale as the single-storey cottage. Many of these were of a higher standard than those built fifty years earlier, being larger and, usually, with at least two rooms. Some had a second bedroom, and a scullery and pantry, as did those in Chapel Row, Grange Moor (144) (see Fig 42).

Typical two-storeyed mill workers' houses also provided more accommodation than had similar, earlier, textile workers' cottages. Generally, a greater proportion of cottages was provided with two bedrooms than before and many had three. Although the proportion of cottages with a separate scullery on the ground floor did not increase significantly, the vast majority of houses built in the second

Plate 119. Deputy Row, Outwood

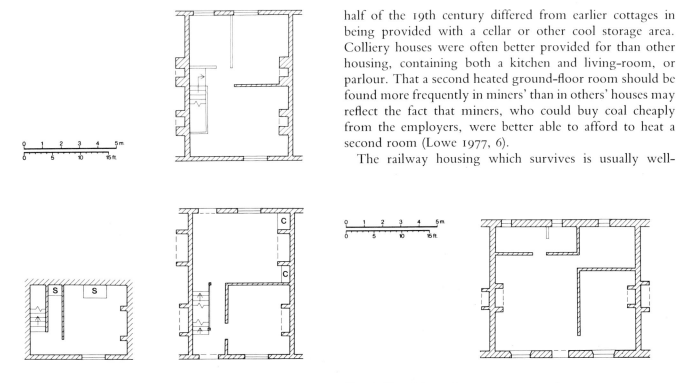

half of the 19th century differed from earlier cottages in being provided with a cellar or other cool storage area. Colliery houses were often better provided for than other housing, containing both a kitchen and living-room, or parlour. That a second heated ground-floor room should be found more frequently in miners' than in others' houses may reflect the fact that miners, who could buy coal cheaply from the employers, were better able to afford to heat a second room (Lowe 1977, 6).

The railway housing which survives is usually well-

Fig 41. Deputy Row, Outwood

Fig 42. Chapel Row, Grange Moor

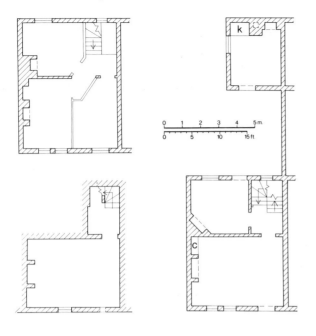

Fig 43. No.40, Midland Terrace, Bradford

designed, company houses generally being built as throughs. In those at Midland Terrace, Bradford (10) and Railway Terrace, Stanley (128) the first floor was divided by ingeniously shaped partitions in order to provide three bedrooms, two of them heated (Figs 43, 44). In Midland Terrace the houses contained two heated living-rooms and also had an individual wash-house in the back yard (Pl 120), while at Railway Terrace, Stanley, the back yards have extremely high walls, so giving the desired privacy to the conveniences within them (Pl 121). At Low Moor the housing built by the Lancashire and Yorkshire Railway (93) was provided with only two bedrooms, but by the late 19th century railway housing generally contained three bedrooms, a living-room, a kitchen, and sometimes a scullery as well (PRO Rail 491/360).[9]

Estate housing was also influenced by changing concepts of acceptable standards. A number of estate cottages were built in Aberford in the 19th century. In the earlier ones it seems that appearance was an important consideration. One typical pair, along Bunker's Hill (82), was built in the picturesque style, the first-floor windows, whose design contributes much to the picturesque look, providing but

Plate 120.
Wash-house,
Midland Terrace, Bradford

Plate 121 (*above*).
Rear of Railway Terrace,
Outwood

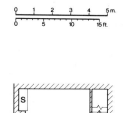
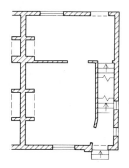
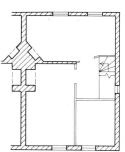

Fig 44 (*left*).
Railway Terrace, Outwood

Plate 122. Estate cottages, Bunkers Hill, Aberford

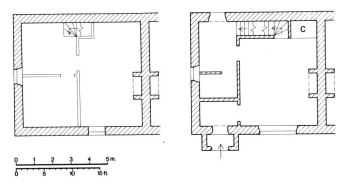

Fig 45. Estate cottages, Bunkers Hill, Aberford

poor lighting to the bedrooms (Pl 122, Fig 45). Another row of estate cottages, built in Mytholmroyd (93) in 1853, also looks impressive but again is unsatisfactory in design (Pl 123, Fig 46). The cottages were of the basic one-up/one-down plan; with a loft which could be used to provide additional sleeping accommodation. The worst feature of design was the fact that the cottages were built above a farm building used for cattle accommodation, and reputed to have been used as a slaughter-house. During the second half of the 19th century contemporary ideas on required housing standards seem to have had a greater influence. Appearance was still important, but planning improved. The estate

Plate 123 (*above*).
Ewood Cottages,
Mytholmroyd

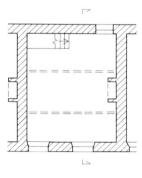

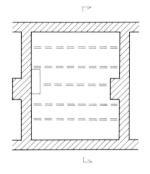

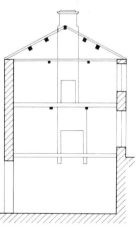

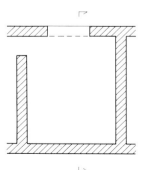

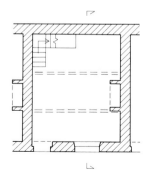

Fig 46 (*right*).
Estate cottages, Midgley Road,
Mytholmroyd

Plate 124. Bridge Cottages, Aberford

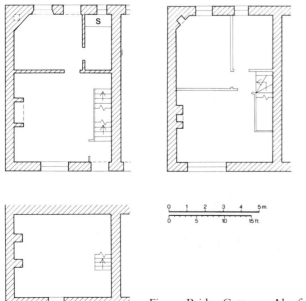

Fig 47. Bridge Cottages, Aberford

Plate 125. Privies to rear of Bridge Cottages, Aberford

cottages in Aberford culminated in 1896 with Bridge Cottages (82), which incorporate many elements of model housing, the seven houses being throughs, with front gardens and their own privies (Pls 124, 125). The front door opened into a lobby, off which ran the stairs and each house was provided with the requisite number of rooms (living-room, scullery, and three bedrooms), sufficient storage space (cellar and pantry) and conveniences (set-pot, two heated bedrooms) (Fig 47). In addition, the houses were gas-lit and built soundly, use being made of the latest technical improvements.

Notes to Chapter 6
[1] It has been pointed out that the Poor Law Commission which submitted this report was trying to stimulate action to improve workers' housing and that the report may therefore have been biased to achieve this end (Rimmer 1963, 182).
[2] The competition for urban housing plans held in 1860 by the Leeds local committee of the Royal Agricultural Society, for example, specified that developments should bring a return of 7½ per cent (*Builder* 1861, 62).
[3] In Leeds, Robert Baker, the medical officer of health, stressed in his reports of the 1840s the link between outbreaks of cholera and areas of inadequate and insanitary housing (Beresford 1971, 111).
[4] Contemporaries believed that disease was carried by an airborne miasma and that circulation of air would prevent the formation of such miasmas.
[5] Halifax 1869, 13; Halifax 1893, 8; Leeds 1878, 6; Leeds 1901, 11.
[6] Bradford 1865, 5; Bradford 1875, 18; Halifax 1869, 14; Halifax 1893, 11; Leeds 1901, 77.
[7] In Bradford the bye-laws of 1865 required carriageways to be 35 feet (10.68 m) wide and non-carriageways to be 24 feet (7.32 m) wide. In 1870 the specifications for carriageways were increased to 42 feet (12.18 m) (Bradford 1865, 3; Bradford 1870, 3–4).
[8] In Bradford the average weekly rent rose from between 2s 6d and 3s for a two-bedroomed back-to-back in the mid 19th century to between 4s and 4s 6d for a larger two- or three-bedroomed back-to-back in the 1880s (Cudworth 1977, 58).
[9] Not all railway housing was of such good quality. A survey made in 1863 of the North Eastern Railway Company's housing shows that many of the employees lived in poorly constructed dwellings badly in need of repair (PRO RAIL 527/1145).

CHAPTER 7

BUILDERS AND HOUSE DESIGN, 1880–1920

House building activity continued to increase in the latter years of the 19th century and the early years of the 20th century, a trend which had, however, been reversed by the outbreak of the Great War. In urban areas sustained population growth was reflected in the ever increasing amount of terrace housing, the vast majority of which was built by speculative builders. In Leeds it would appear that builders, or building companies, acquired plots of land which they then developed street by street, each being built up in short sections. It was in this manner that the firm of Joseph Pullan and Sons built up the Marleys and Nosters (Marley Terrace, Grove, View, Place and Street, Noster Street, Place, View and Hill), in Beeston between 1896 and 1908 (Pl 126; Fig 48). Further north, in Holbeck, the Farndale Brothers operated in the same way to build up Runswick Place, Runswick Terrace and Runswick Street between 1895 and 1897 (Pl 127), and all around Leeds there were similar developments: in Headingley B and W Walmsley Brothers, built up Harold Place and Harold Grove, Thornville Road, Green, Terrace, Place and Row in the 1890s, followed by the Hessles, Thornville Crescent and Meadow View (WYAS Leeds Building Plan Indices).

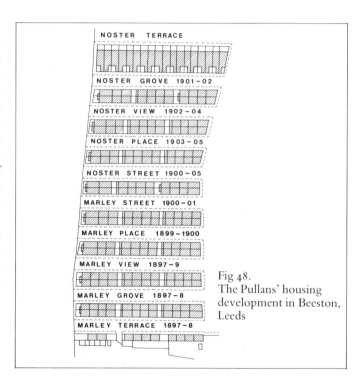

Fig 48.
The Pullans' housing development in Beeston, Leeds

Plate 126. The Pullans' development (the Marleys and Nosters), Beeston, Leeds

Plate 127.
No. 22, Runswick Street,
Holbeck, Leeds

Most builders, however, operated on a smaller scale, individual streets being developed by a number of builders in a more piece-meal fashion. In Bradford this was the way in which an area north of the Leeds Road was developed. Here, although certain builders were responsible for constructing large numbers of houses, their properties were distributed throughout the area, streets being built up by different combinations of builders. Amongst others Joseph Marshall was active in Granton Street, Greenhill Lane, Lapage Street and Rochester Street, whilst Stephen Johnson operated in Greenhill Lane, Harewood Street, Lapage Street and Rochester Street (WYAS Bradford Building Plans Indices).

In some cases speculative builders constructed houses to rent rather than to sell. To this day the Pullans rent out the estate of houses which the firm built in Beeston, but in such instances there was no difference between houses built to rent and those built for sale.

This period saw an acceleration of the tendency for building societies to finance large speculative house-building projects, a departure from their original intention of lending to the small-scale investor. The loans that they now made to their smaller investors tended to be for the purchase of ready-built houses rather than, as formerly, to provide finance for them to build their own properties. One such investor was Walter Hunbrods, a chemist from Kirkstall, Leeds, who in 1900 borrowed £2,500 from the Leeds Permanent Building Society in order to buy six houses and two houses with shops in Runswick Street and Terrace (LPBS Surveyors' Book 1900, September 26). These houses had been built three years previously by the speculative builders Joseph and William Farndale (Kelly's Trade Directory 1893, 1899; Leeds Building Plan indices 1895, 1896), and there are numerous examples of similar transactions (Halifax Building Society, 1897–1913; LPBS Surveyors' Book 1900). Building Societies had, therefore, become increasingly important in the house-building trade both enabling houses to be built and then assisting prospective occupants to purchase them.

Employers continued to build workers' housing, although by the end of the century it was not the mill owners but the coal companies who were the principal providers. This was due partly to the increasing tendency for textile mills to be located in areas which were already built-up, where speculators and others were available and willing to provide housing, thereby removing the necessity for employers to do so. In the coal industry, on the other hand, pits continued to be located in relatively isolated rural areas, necessitating the provision of housing by the employers. The continued growth in the average size of individual workings was matched by an expansion in the size of their workforces, resulting in the need to provide housing on a commensurately large scale (Walters 1927, v).

HOUSE DESIGN

The prevalent type of workers housing in this period continued to be the terraced house of either the through or back-to-back variety.

Through house plans had become standardized to a large degree, the good average type of 'through' on which the Bradford Equitable Building Society gave loans in 1898 included a living-room, a scullery, four bedrooms, a cellar, a water closet and an ash-hole (Lumb 1951, facing 26, 34). In other throughs there might be only two or three bedrooms, but there were few other variations. Throughs continued to be built in both rural and urban areas, as densely as possible where land was valuable. The proportion of such houses built increased while that of back-to-backs diminished. The latter were provided in decreasing quantities but continued to be built in the early years of the 20th century, supplying cheaper accommodation for less affluent workers. Speculative builders used different types of house plan to appeal to people with varied incomes. In Headingley, Leeds, for example, one of Walmsley Brothers' developments ranged from through houses in Hessle View (which had sculleries, bay windows, entrance corridors and small front gardens), to the smaller four-bedroom through houses in Thornville Crescent, and to the three-bedroomed back-to-backs in Thornville Mount (Fig 49).

Back-to-backs remained a common type of workers' house until the national ban on them of 1909; as with the through plan the accommodation offered in back-to-backs had become standardized to a large extent by the late 19th century. By the 1890s they were invariably provided with a basement or cellar, a living room and scullery on the ground floor, two bedrooms on the first floor and, more often than not, a third bedroom in the attic. For examples in Bradford and Leeds see Figs 49–53. Different bye-laws required conveniences and yards to be provided and arranged in

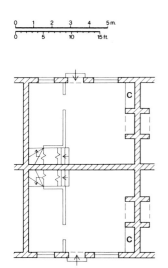
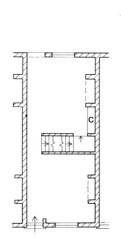
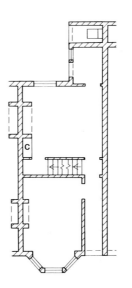

Fig 49.
Walmsley Brothers' housing,
Headingley, Leeds
(a) Thornville Mount;
(b) 11, Thornville Crescent;
(c) 9, Hessle View

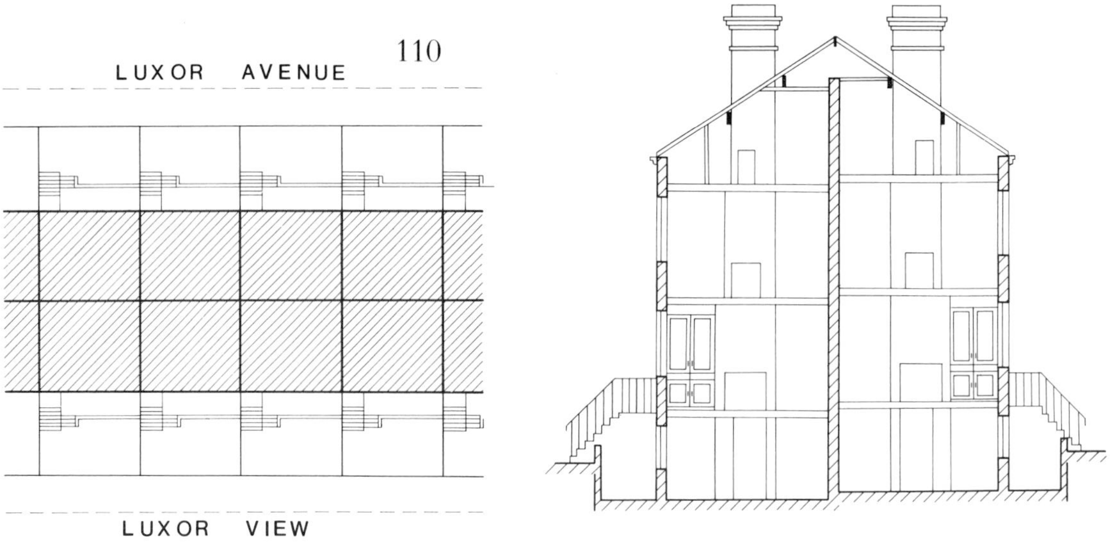

Fig 50.
Luxor View,
Harehills, Leeds.
This and Figs. 51–53
illustrate late 19th-
century back-to-back
plan types

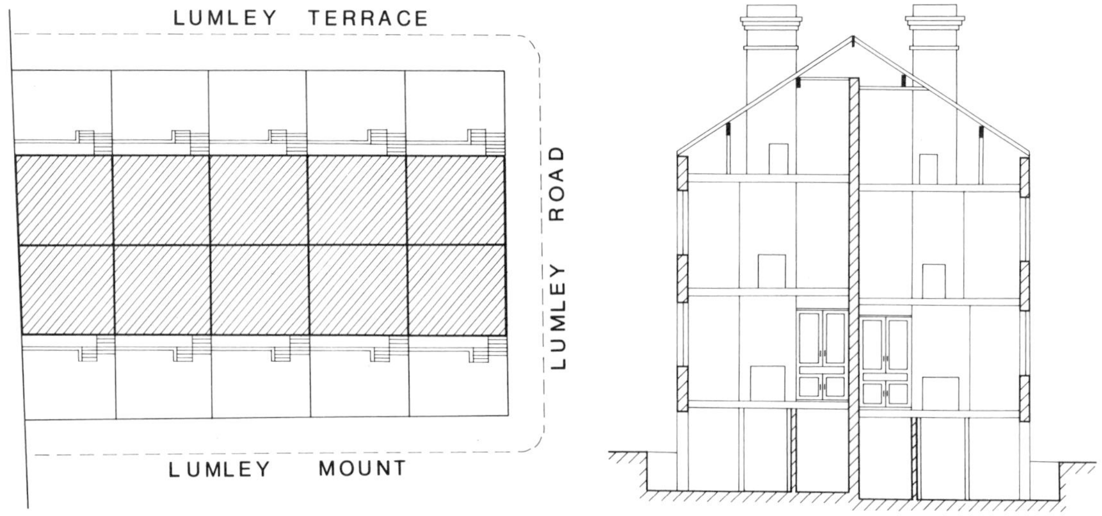

LUXOR AVENUE

LUXOR VIEW

Fig 51.
Lumley Mount,
Headingley, Leeds

LUMLEY TERRACE

LUMLEY ROAD

LUMLEY MOUNT

Fig 52.
Southampton Street,
Bradford

SOUTHAMPTON STREET

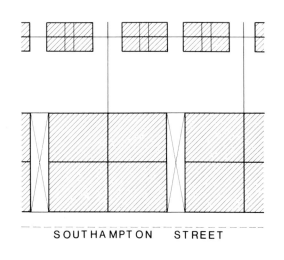

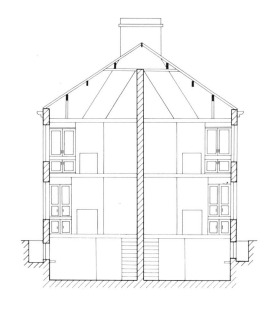

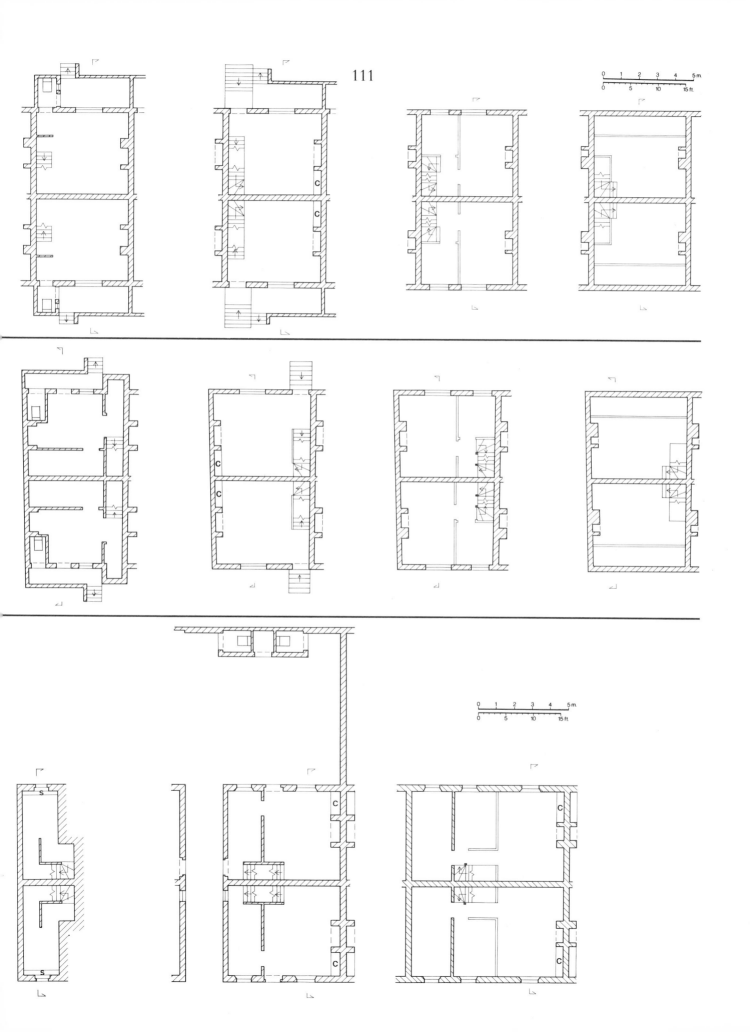

Fig 53. William Street, Headingley, Leeds

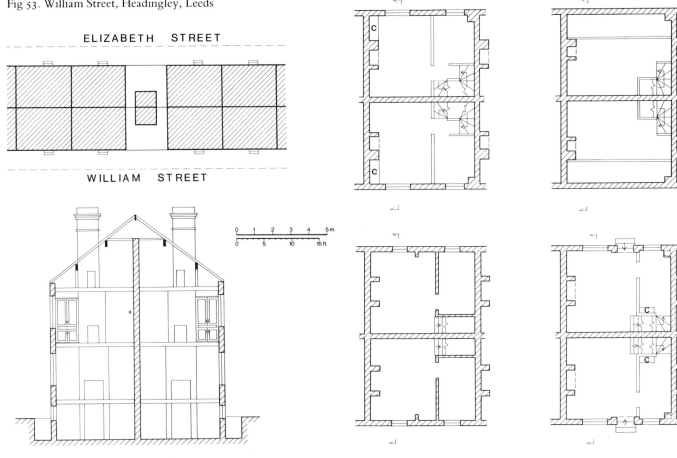

ELIZABETH STREET

WILLIAM STREET

Plate 128.
William Street,
Headingley, Leeds

Plate 129.
Southampton Street,
Bradford

different ways, however, affecting the composition of blocks of back-to-backs. In Keighley and Morley the bye-laws stipulated that there be free circulation of air to the side and front of each back-to-back, making it impossible to build more than four in a block (Mair 1910, and Muthesius 1982, 117). In Leeds the bye-laws allowed back-to-backs to be built in larger blocks of up to eight houses, punctuated by shared yards (Pl 128). In Bradford, on the other hand, back-to-backs could be built in longer terraces with shared back yards, access being provided to the dwellings at the rear by a side passage between every second house (Pl 129).

Shortly before the national ban on back-to-back building, opposition of housing reformers to them had grown in strength and stimulated attempts to provide improved yet equally cheap forms of housing. Based on evidence taken from several towns in the West Riding, including Dewsbury, Huddersfield, Leeds and Morley, Dr Darra Mair proved to his own and the Government's satisfaction that there was a higher mortality rate amongst those living in back-to-backs than in through-ventilated dwellings (Mair 1910, 7–8, 29). In 1890 the Bradford architects Mawson and Hudson in promoting a new house-type presented a strong case against even the better built back-to-backs, reiterating that these gave no through ventilation. They also attacked the practice of providing privies and ash-houses in a shared yard which they believed resulted in a lack of privacy for those waiting to use them and in danger to children going out to them at night. Further, it was pointed out that where the shared yard was situated behind a terrace the rear dwellings had a view only of these conveniences, and families eating their meals were seated opposite privies which might be in use. During the summer, moreover, the

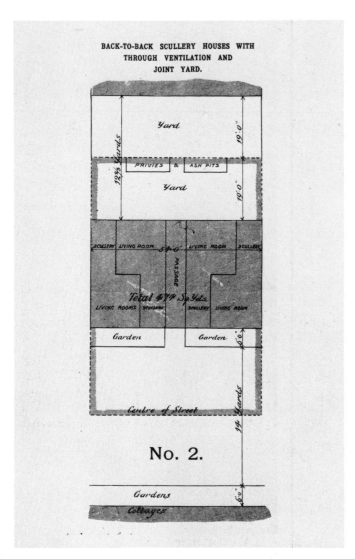

Plate 130. Mawson and Hudson's through-by-lights plan

smell from privies and ash-pits affected the rear dwellings.

Mawson and Hudson's alternative to back-to-backs was to build terraced houses with an interlocking L-shaped plan (see Pl 130). These houses, which were known locally as through-by-lights, could be built on land as economically as back-to-backs but provided a through draught. At the turn of the century Mawson and Hudson tried to persuade the Bradford Corporation to sponsor houses of this type:

> Gentlemen, in July 1890, we had the pleasure to introduce to your notice (what we thought) an improved plan for building back-to-back cottages, whereby a through current of air from front to back could be obtained, and which could not be got in the present style of building. And, in addition to this, a great advantage is gained by bringing the housewife from the back living room to the front scullery overlooking the street while household duties are being performed, thereby making the houses healthier and more cheerful in every respect . . . We may also add these back-to-back cottages in the new system are nearly equal to through houses with their front and back streets for approaches (Mawson and Hudson 1893, 3).

In his book on workers' housing of 1866, James Hole illustrated some model cottages built in Leeds as through-by-lights (Pl 131), but it appears that the idea of building on these lines had not been adopted widely by the time Mawson and Hudson made their proposals. At about that time, however, examples start to be found. Number 8 Elliot Street, Shipley (113), is one of a group of twenty-four built c.1905 (Pl 132, Fig 54). Although this type of house does not seem to have been built in large numbers, there are other examples, some at Loscoe, for example, being built slightly earlier (JGLS 1903, 361). The reason for through-by-lights not being more widely adopted is obscure; it may be

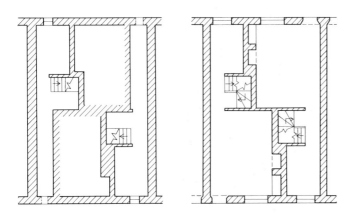
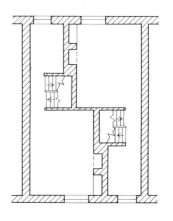
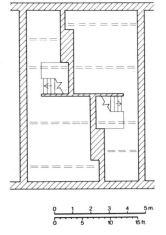

Fig 54. Through-by-lights, 8, Elliot Street, Shipley

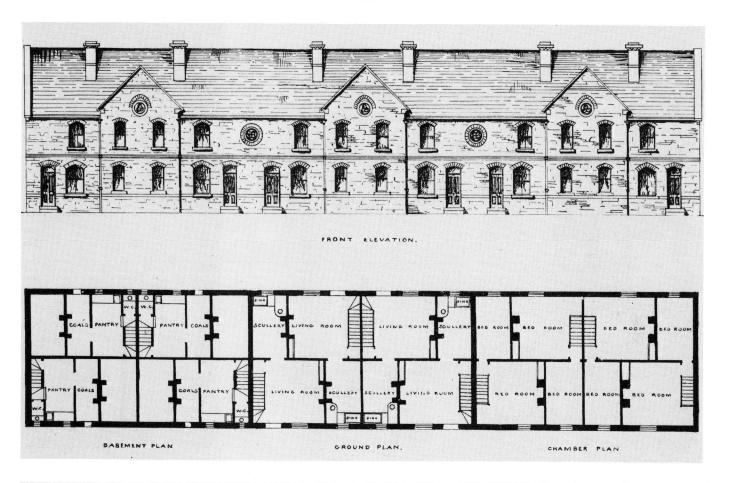

FRONT ELEVATION.

BASEMENT PLAN   GROUND PLAN.   CHAMBER PLAN

Plate 131 (*above*).
Through-by-light cottages,
New Wortley, Leeds

Plate 132 (*left*).
Through-by-lights,
Elliot Street, Shipley

Plate 133. Colliery housing, Whitwood, designed by Voysey (1904): general view

Plate 134. Colliery housing, Whitwood: elevation, plans and sections

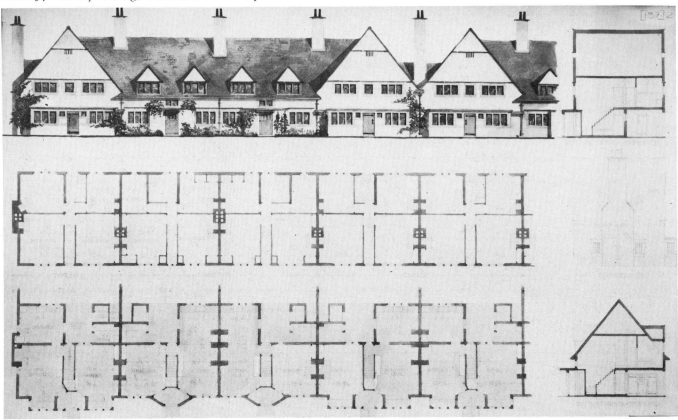

Plate 135. Colliery housing, Whitwood: frontage to street

because, just as the plan was evolved, there was a slump in all housebuilding. Before this type could oust the traditional back-to-back, moreover, all accommodation of that nature was banned by national legislation.

Mawson and Hudson's proposed through-by-lights houses were, however, in practice, simply a slightly modified traditional back-to-back plan type. More innovatory was a terrace of nineteen dwellings built at Whitwood in 1904–05. C F A Voysey was commissioned by the coal company of Henry Briggs and Son to design the terrace, which was intended for colliery officials in the company's employ (Pls 133–6). Contact between the Briggs family and Voysey seems to have been first made in 1898, in which year Voysey designed a house (Broadleys) for Briggs at Windermere (Simpson, 1979). The terrace was built to a high standard structurally, architecturally and in terms of the accommodation it provided, although Voysey complained that 'The Company found it necessary to build the houses so cheaply that architectural superintendence was perforce left out of court, (Symonds 1976, 44). The treatment of the terrace, with its rough-cast rendering and broken roof line, is characteristic of Voysey's style. As such it marked a departure from the more strictly functional tradition in which aesthetic considerations were usually limited to the embellishment of external features and the use of mass-produced applied ornamentation (Pl 137). Voysey's Whit-

Plate 136. Colliery housing, Whitwood: rear view

Plate 137. Decorative details:

Far left:
(a) Doorway, Granton Street, Bradford

Left:
(b) Bay window, Arthington Terrace, Leeds

Below left:
(c) Window, Luxor Street, Leeds

Below:
(d) Iron railings, Arthington Terrace, Leeds

Right:
(e) Decorated window and eaves, Luxor Street, Leeds

Below:
(f) Decorated eaves, Garnet Road, Leeds

Below right:
(g) Air brick, New Crofton

Plate 138. First-floor rendering, Walton

The Havercroft housing was built after the Great War by the Industrial Housing Association, an independent national body established by the colliery companies in an attempt to alleviate the post-war shortage of accommodation for miners by building housing for them on a non-profit making basis. In West Yorkshire two estates were built, at Havercroft and Upton, the houses reflecting the association's concern to provide a high standard of housing incorporating the most modern contemporary ideas on all aspects of design, facilities and environmental planning.

By the time that the Industrial Housing Association began building in the 1920s, the consensus of opinion as to the amount of accommodation requisite for a family formulated in the second half of the 19th century had begun to come increasingly under attack. The demand of various early 20th-century architects and housing reformers that workers' houses should comprise three bedrooms, a living-room, a scullery, a larder, a fuel store and a privy or water closet echoed that of their 19th-century predecessors (Cornes 1905, v; Cutler 1896, 7; Board of Agriculture 1913, cited in Swenarton 1981, 42). The requirement for three bedrooms was, however, met more frequently in the early 20th century than formerly, although there were still many instances of dwellings such as 41 Woodbine Street, Ossett (103), which, while being well-built in other respects, were provided with only two.

Architects and housing reformers continued to write about the need to provide an adequate water supply, sanitary system and drainage, to light a house well both naturally and artificially, to heat and ventilate it sufficiently, and to provide adequate food, fuel and storage spaces (Cornes 1905, vviii; Cutler 1896, 14–16; Walters 1927, 192).

wood houses were very much an exception to the rule, the austere and regimented terrace rows built by Lord St Oswald for his miners at New Crofton in the following year being more representative of miners' housing of the period. The use of rough-cast and pebble-dash rendering, usually of the upper floor only was, however adopted increasingly, the pale-coloured rendering contrasting with the red brick below and alleviating its otherwise harsh monotony. Early examples of first-floor rendering are to be seen at housing developments at Havercroft and Walton (Pls 138, 139).

Plate 139. First-floor rendering, Ryehill, Havercroft

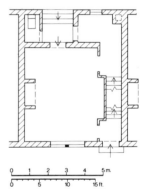

Plate 140 (*above*).
Housing at Crystal
Bedding Works,
Union Street,
Heckmondwike

Fig 55.
No.43, Union Street,
Heckmondwike

Plate 141. Union Street, Heckmondwike: two houses

That these ideas had some impact is shown in the more general provision in workers' houses of a water supply, ash-houses and gas-lighting. Fixed wall cupboards in the living-rooms, which had become a standard feature earlier in the 19th century, were becoming common in upper rooms by the later years of the century. Storage facilities were also improved by the more frequent provision of larger closets, which had begun to be provided in workers' houses in the mid-19th century, though they still occurred in relatively small numbers. Larders and fuel stores became standard features of house plans provided, if not in a cellar, then as a pantry and outside coal store (as was the case in the houses at New Crofton (28) and at Union Street, Heckmondwike (47)) (Pls 140, 141, Fig 55; Pls 143, 144, Fig 56).

122

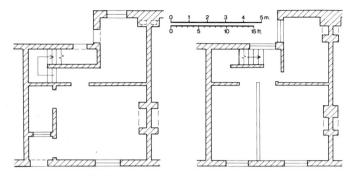

Fig 56. Colliery housing, New Crofton

One of the most significant developments in this period was the increasing provision of both water closets and baths. Once the water closet had been developed to an adequate standard it became important to advocates of model housing that this should be the type of toilet supplied. Ideally they wished it to be placed within the house walls, both to provide maximum privacy (Cornes 1905, viii) and to prevent water freezing in the cistern (Mawson and Hudson 1893, 11). On the issue of providing water closets speculative builders were almost as keen as the proponents of model housing for, by placing them within the body of the house back-to-backs could be built without the shared yards formerly provided to contain such conveniences, thereby allowing denser development of building land. Water closets began to come into general use around the turn of the 19th century, the building company of Joseph Pullan and Sons, for example, introducing them on their Beeston housing development in 1900. Houses in Marley Street and Noster Street were the first to be supplied with them although they were still positioned in shared yards (WYAS Leeds, Building Plans).

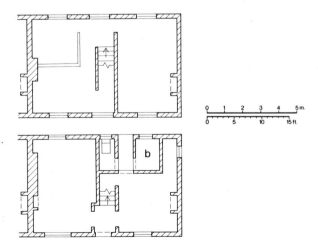

Fig 57. No.23, East Street, Havercroft

A plan which made use of the water closet to allow denser development and one commonly adopted in Leeds in the early years of the 20th century, was to locate it in the basement. This was done in the back-to-backs in Lumley Mount, built in 1901 (Fig 51). Alternatively, the water closet was positioned under steps which led up to the house door, a practice which was also common in Leeds (Fig 50). That there were still problems with odour seems to be apparent from the fact that access to closets remained external, not only in speculatively-built houses, but also in better-built houses, such as those in Union Street, Heckmondwike (47), and at Havercroft (48) (Fig 57).

Housing reformers also favoured the provision of a bath (Cornes 1905 v). By the later 19th century baths, connected to a hot and cold water supply, were beginning to be provided in workers' houses. Generally, the bath was positioned in the scullery and covered by a wooden lid when not in use. This was the arrangement in the majority of the Pullans' houses at Beeston and in the colliery houses in Garden Terrace, Painthorpe (27). Housing reformers ideally wanted the bath to be placed in a separate room (Workmens' National Housing Council 1917 and Tudor Walters' Report, 1918, both cited in Swenarton 1981, 91, 88, 109). This was done in superior workers' houses, including those at Whitwood, and some on the Pullans' Beeston housing development (Pl 142, Fig 58) and in some of the housing built by model builders, such as the colliery houses at Havercroft (48) and Walton (150). In view of the dirtiness of the occupation it is not surprising that miners' houses were amongst the first to be equipped with bathrooms (Walters 1927, 30), but not until the 1930s were bathrooms more generally provided.

Whereas in the mid-19th century housing reformers had been concerned to establish an acceptable minimum standard of accommodation, in the later 19th and early 20th centuries their attention increasingly encompassed considerations of internal design as well. One of their concerns was how best to arrange internal fitments in order to economize on the effort of the user. The Industrial Housing Association was concerned that

> In the planning of the houses consideration should be given to the convenience of the housewife, and the position of the pantry, working range, kitchen dresser, and sink in relation to the number of footsteps that have to be taken to perform the day's work (Walters 1927, 192).

The Association was also concerned as to whether to build bathrooms downstairs, where they could be used by home-coming miners without dirtying the rest of the house, or upstairs, where they were more convenient for women and children (Walters 1927, 30). In the miners' houses in

West Yorkshire the bathroom, where there was one, tended to be situated downstairs. Another area of discussion was how best to provide privacy for the users of water closets and bathrooms. Although these continued to be reached by an external door, maximum privacy could be ensured by supplying access from the back door porch. This was done at Brooklands Road, Walton (150), and Union Street, Heckmondwike (47). Alternatively, access could be given off an internal passage leading to the back door, as was the case at Havercroft, Hemsworth (48). Housing reformers continued to advocate entrance into a lobby rather than directly into the living-room (Cutler 1896, 15). This feature was provided in more houses than formerly, as also was a window to light the stair. Another contemporary requirement echoing earlier views was that the stair should rise from a lobby or hall rather than from the living-room (Cornes 1905, vviii), a feature which was incorporated in an increasing number of workers' houses in order to exclude dirt and draughts.

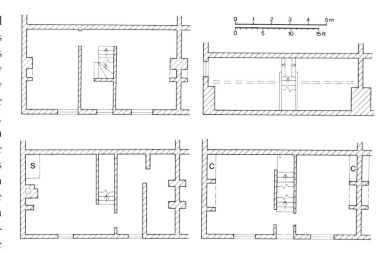

Fig 58. No. 17, Noster Street, Beeston, Leeds

Plate 142.
No. 17, Noster Street, Leeds

Plate 143 (*left*).
Miners' housing,
New Crofton

Fig 59 (*below*).
Colliery Housing,
New Crofton

Plate 144. New Crofton: two houses

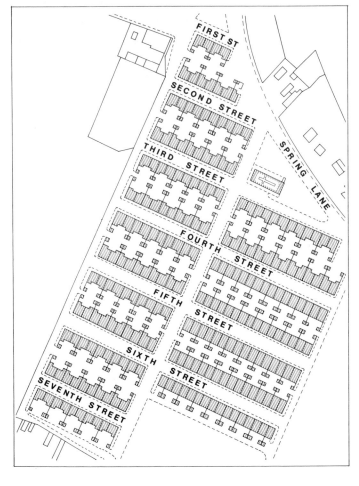

It was in this period that the ideas of housing reformers and propagandist of the garden city like Ebenezer Howard, Barry Parker and Raymond Unwin, began to be reflected in the design of an increasing number of housing developments. The basic premise of these writers was that dwellings need not be built 'in a monotonous row, nor need they be ugly' (Cutler 1896, 8). Instead, it was argued, they should be built at a low density in short rows, if in rows at all, and surrounded by a reasonable area of open space.

Plate 145 (*above*).
Ryhill, Havercroft

Plate 146 (*left*).
Housing at Walton

Villages of the type built at New Crofton, with its grid-iron plan, were replaced by developments with a more open layout, like that at Havercroft, where there was great variety both in the appearance of houses and in their grouping (compare Pls 143, 144 and Figs 56 and 57). The uniform appearance of New Crofton was underlined by the unimaginative naming of the streets from First Street to Seventh Street. Though only twenty years separate the two developments, the design of individual houses at each also reflects the advance which had occurred in housing concepts. The Crofton colliery cottages, described by one contemporary as 'a very good example of scullery cottages with three bedrooms' (John Goodchild Loan Collection: County Medical Officer's Report 1906, 21), were directly descended from a long tradition of terraced miners' housing. The houses at Havercroft on the other hand, with their internal water closets and bathrooms, two living-rooms, spacious layouts and rough-cast walls, reflect the broader approach of architects and builders to the design of workers' housing (Pls 145, 146; Figs 59, 60).

The housing at New Crofton, Havercroft and Walton was all built by colliery owners for their employees. Plans for similar developments for textile workers were not forthcoming, although S and C Firth of Cellars Clough Mills, Marsden, drew up plans for a garden-city development of 169 houses for their employees, to be supplemented with allotments, parkland and playgrounds. The scheme had to be dropped, however, when war broke out in 1914 and as a result of the subsequent recession in the textile industry was never carried out (Cellar Clough Mills papers).

One noticeable feature of early 20th-century model housing was the provision of large gardens or allotments. The Havercroft houses had large front and back gardens, while at Crofton the miners could rent allotments. Contemporary housing reformers valued these gardens and allotments for the same reasons as their mid 19th-century predecessors, believing that the land provided a healthy form of recreation and could supplement the owner's income in times of unemployment. (Rowntree and Pigou 1914, 12; Walters 1927, 25.) The 19th-century belief that builders of large-scale housing developments should provide educational and other communal facilities continued

Fig 60. Ryhill, Havercroft

into the early 20th century (Cutler 1896, 9). Sir Tudor Walters explained how the Industrial Housing Association provided shops, pubs and sites for places for worship and institutes (Walters 1927, 25, 27), while Henry Briggs and Son, built a workman's institute next to Whitwood Terrace (now the Rising Sun public house), and contributed to the building of other institutes and schools. (University of Leeds MS 160, 82, 20, 55, 72) (Pl 147). The continuation of these earlier 19th-century ideals, combining with the new concepts introduced at the turn of the century, resulted in a qualitative improvement of much workers' housing, whether built by speculators or employers.

Right: Plate 147. Arthur Currer Briggs Memorial Hall, Whitwood

CHAPTER 8

LOCAL AUTHORITY INVOLVEMENT
AND THE ORIGINS OF COUNCIL HOUSING

Bye-Laws

During the second half of the 19th century local government became increasingly involved in the issue of workers' housing, its intervention usually taking the form of regulative bye-laws. By the 1880s, however, it had become apparent that local bye-laws were not having as great an effect in improving poor-quality housing as had been hoped. The ineffectiveness of many bye-laws was reflected in the frequency with which they were reiterated and was partly due to the large scale of the problems with which they were intended to deal. Ineffectiveness was also the result of the unwillingness of local authorities to incur unpopularity and so risk displacement from office. This they might do by increasing rates to finance large-scale improvements or by acting too forcibly against those contravening the bye-laws. A further problem with the bye-law system by the 1880s was its complexity. So much legislation had been passed, frequently amending and re-amending earlier regulations, that it had become difficult to comprehend. Following an enquiry into the condition of workers' housing by a Royal Commission, and in an attempt to improve this situation, the government passed the Housing of the Working Classes Act in 1890. The aim of this legislation was not so much to introduce new building requirements as to consolidate and clarify those which already existed.

Following on from this act, local authorities reviewed their own housing regulations. In Halifax the Corporation began work in 1888 on a new set of bye-laws which came into effect in 1893. The new bye-laws generally made the same stipulations as before about building standards, street widths, ceiling heights, windows, ventilation, toilets and ash places. Some extensions to the rules were effected, both at this time and during another flurry of bye-law legislation in 1902. Damp-proof courses, for example, were required in new buildings and in Leeds for the first time one privy or water closet was demanded for each house.

By the early 20th century bye-laws had come to affect most aspects of house building. Ironically, some contemporary architects now began to express the view that requirements were too stringent, so deterring cottage building and exacerbating the problems of overcrowding. In 1905 James Cornes felt that

> No-one could condemn wholesale the bye-laws which have done so much to promote sound and sanitary buildings, but there is no doubt that in many districts they prevent the building of cottages suitable to the needs of the local population and restrict the use of materials which are to hand (Cornes 1905, 124; see also Daunton 1983, 288–9).

Bradford Corporation encountered problems of this nature in 1907 when it first tried to obtain planning approval to build tenemented blocks. The Health and Sanitary Committee refused to allow their construction on the grounds that they did not conform with existing building regulations (WYAS, Bradford, Faxfleet Street Papers, 1907). This was hardly surprising, given that the existing regulations did not deal with tenements. In the event a full-scale enquiry had to be held before the plans were eventually passed in 1908 (Pye 1981, Blc). Problems were also encountered with building regulations when it was decided to construct low-density housing along garden-city lines. In order to make such projects financially viable, economies were made on road-making costs by providing narrow roads and cul-de-sacs, their narrowness more than offset by the provision of roadside verges and front gardens (Swenarton 1981, 15). To do this the developer needed to obtain exemption from the bye-laws which required broad, inter-connecting streets. It is not surprising, therefore, that such housing was generally provided by local authorities or other influential bodies (such as the Industrial Housing Association). Not only were speculators less interested in providing this sort of development, their paramount considerations still being the cost of building land and the desire to build as densely as possible, but also it would have been harder for them to acquire bye-law exemptions. For local authorities, on the other hand, this increasingly became less of a problem. During the First World War national legislation exempted government housing schemes from building requirements and in 1919 this exemption was extended to those of local authorities (Swenarton 1981, 15).

THE DEVELOPMENT OF HOUSING POLICY

The beginning of direct involvement in house building by local authorities was perhaps one of the most significant developments in the field of workers' housing in the late 19th and early 20th centuries. Legislation passed in the second half of the 19th century had failed to eliminate the poorest quality housing since, not being retrospective, it could do little to improve conditions in older properties which had deteriorated into slums. Every town had its 'unhealthy areas' (Pls 106, 107), reports made in the early years of the 20th century revealing that many people were still living in insanitary and overcrowded accommodation, as for example at Pontefract.[1] In the interest of public health the government was keen to see those areas improved and tried to stimulate local authorities to take appropriate action by giving encouragement and financial assistance.

One method by which local authorities could improve areas of insanitary housing was to undertake clearance schemes. Provisions were made enabling them to do so, but from the increasing grants of freedom from restrictions on such projects it appears that local authorities were not eager to embark on such schemes. In 1875 they were given the power to clear areas of dwellings considered unfit for human habitation, provided that they rehoused displaced persons on the same site and sold any houses built in the process within ten years. In 1879 the requirement that people be rehoused on site was removed, in 1882 only half of those displaced had to be rehoused, and in 1890 this requirement was removed altogether (Merrett 1979, 307, 309).

Despite this legislative encouragement, the clearance work undertaken by the authorities was minimal. In Leeds only one such operation was carried out between 1870 and 1878. This scheme cleared and developed a mere 3 acres in the Union Street area, where the late 18th and early 19th-century housing provided by Richard Paley and other speculators had long since deteriorated into an 'unhealthy area'. Despite the small scale of this project the clearance and demolition work alone cost the council £25,000 (Lupton 1906, 11). The costs involved, however, discouraged other such schemes.

In 1890 the government offered local authorities loan facilities (Allen 1901, 35, 36). This appears to have been the stimulus behind a change in council policy both in Leeds, where several schemes were undertaken in the 1890s, and in Bradford. The largest project in Leeds was the clearance of 66¾ acres of slum land in the York Road and Quarry Hill area, begun in 1895 (Lupton 1906, 5, 6). A few years later demand began in Bradford for a similar project to clear unsatisfactory housing and provide new accommodation in the Longlands area (Brockway 1946, 48). The Leeds and Bradford clearance schemes were undertaken against a background of extremely vocal controversy over whether or not local authorities should become involved in such ventures. Opponents of the schemes questioned the necessity and the right of local authorities becoming involved or the value of their doing so. In Leeds, for example, Alderman Lupton felt that speculative builders could meet housing requirements satisfactorily and that large expenditure of rate-payers' money on such schemes was unjustified (Lupton 1906, 14–15). By the early 20th century, however, the majority of local councillors accepted the need for action, since the shortage of accommodation for workers had by that time become acute.

The reduction in the housing stock available in the early 20th century was partly due to corporation closures of dwellings deemed unfit for human habitation. More significantly, it was the result of a decline in the amount of house building being undertaken. Rising building costs, coupled with the inability of prospective occupants to pay higher prices or rent, supplied speculators with little incentive to provide workers' housing. Other potential investors in housing were discouraged by the same factors and diverted their capital into more profitable and less risky investments (Rowntree and Pigou 1914, 8–12; Daunton 1983, 289).

Even with the involvement of local authorities in providing accommodation, the problem of the housing shortage appeared to some to be insurmountable. In 1905 James Cornes expressed the view that, although schemes for building working-class housing could be made to pay and were being undertaken by individuals, public companies, philanthropic trusts and public authorities,

> practically no headway has been made in dealing with this pressing problem, for not even the inevitable increase of the working-class population of our great towns has been or is being provided for by all the schemes completed and in hand. It, therefore, seems an almost overwhelming and hopeless task, even with all these agencies combined, to provide decent homes for the huge array of workers, whose numbers are constantly increasing (Cornes 1905, xv).

To some contemporaries the answer to the housing shortage was for local authorities to build houses and sell or rent them at subsidized rate (Rowntree and Pigou 1914, 57, 63, 66). This, however, was a contentious issue, others believing that any municipal housing scheme should be self-financing, as had hitherto been required (Cornes 1905, xiv). The question of whether or not to subsidize housing was further complicated by other issues. As the Chairman of Leeds Housing Committee, Alderman Lupton, pointed out in 1906 to provide homes at less than cost price is to give subsidies in aid of wages, and . . . this, by making it possible to work at too low a price, tends to keep down the general rate of wages . . . [which] cannot be desired in the general interest of the community (Lupton 1906, 2).

He also observed that to levy rates to improve areas would increase the rent of other working-class houses by necessitating higher rates on existing housing, which again was undesirable (Lupton 1906, 14; see also Daunton 1983, 290–1). Apart from the difficulties presented by the necessity of making clearance and rehousing schemes self-financing, those authorities which undertook such enterprises faced major problems involved in their implementation and in overcoming local, and frequently internal, opposition. It took four years (1895–9) for Leeds Council to get the York Road clearance scheme in motion and involved negotiations with 153 property owners (Lupton 1906, 6). In Bradford a proposal for the clearance of the Longlands Insanitary Area and the rehousing of its inhabitants took even longer to implement, since it was hindered by the opposition of a number of council members. The Longlands clearance scheme was finally started in 1903, nine years after Councillor Jowett first moved in the council that action be taken (Brockway 1946, 48, 50, 51, 52).

During the 1914–18 war house-building virtually ceased as the supply of materials, building labour and capital diminished. Those who still had the capital or labour available with which to build were discouraged from so doing by the controls which the government imposed on rents. Introduced in order to avoid social unrest, these restricted the prices which could be charged for property and, therefore, provided a final disincentive for investment in housing. By the end of the war it was not only the poorer members of the working class who were suffering from the resultant housing shortage, but also more affluent workers and the middle classes (Finnigan 1980, 113). The acuteness of the housing shortage persuaded many people that subsidies would have to be provided to enable local authorities to improve the situation. By 1914 the idea of subsidizing municipal housing had been accepted by all three major political parties (Orbach 1977, 43). The deterioration of the housing situation during the war strengthened the government's resolve to implement such a subsidy. Spurred on by a fear of civil disorder, the government passed the Housing and Town Planning (or Addison) Act in 1919, hoping to encourage a massive increase in municipal house-building (Swenarton 1981, 79). Under this act local authorities were encouraged to take steps to meet the housing requirements in their areas. Any losses which they incurred through their house-building

activities, and which could not be met by a penny rate, would be covered by the Exchequer (Merrett 1979, 309). This represented considerable, and apparently unlimited, financial assistance. The result was to stimulate ambitious municipal housing projects. In Leeds five building sites were bought, the council proposing to erect 5,800 houses (Finnigan 1980, 117; Leeds Housing Committee 1954, 15). In Bradford also there was a large increase in the number of houses built for the council, particularly in 1921 and 1922 (Geldart 1975, 33). Local authorities were given advice and directions from central government. They were even provided with model house-plans, although they took on architects themselves (twenty-one in Leeds alone), and tended to draw up their own plans (Leeds Housing Committee 1954, 19; Swenarton 1981, 155).

THE IMPLEMENTATION OF HOUSING POLICY

The first houses to be built by local authorities date to the early years of the 20th century. Following the 1890 Housing of the Working Classes Act, authorities were not obliged to provide alternative accommodation when they cleared areas of insanitary housing (Merrett 1979, 309), but in the light of the contemporary accommodation shortage it was recognized that refusal to do so might exacerbate rather than improve the situation. In Leeds the corporation did not undertake any large-scale house-building project until 1907, but this did not mean that it was not involved in the provision of alternative accommodation for inhabitants displaced by clearance schemes. It was intended that these people would be rehoused in property provided by private builders, but on land formerly owned by the council and sold only on condition that workers' housing be built on it. In selling the land the council made a number of requirements as to the standards and design of the new housing and was therefore able to ensure its quality (Lupton 1906, 2).

When Leeds Corporation built houses itself it followed similarly high standards. In 1900 ten houses were built in Derwent Avenue as part of a scheme to improve the Camp Fields area (Lupton 1906, 9; Fig 61). These were designed as throughs, each containing three bedrooms, two of them heated, and had their own water closet and ashbin in a back yard (Fig 62). They were similar to 66 houses built soon afterwards by Bradford Corporation on Faxfleet Street and finished by 1904, being intended to rehouse those displaced by the clearance of Longlands Improvement Area (Bradford 1904, 3). With their spacious accommodation, through ventilation and broad streets they were a great improvement on the dwellings which had been cleared (Pls 148–55).

Within the next ten years Bradford Corporation built a further 89 houses in the Faxfleet Street area. Again these were throughs, each containing two or three bedrooms.

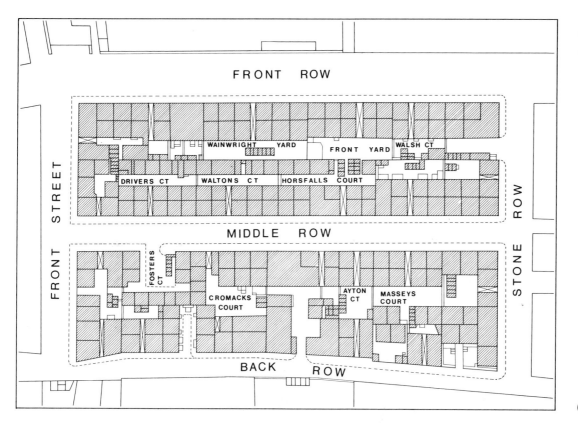

(a) before improvement;

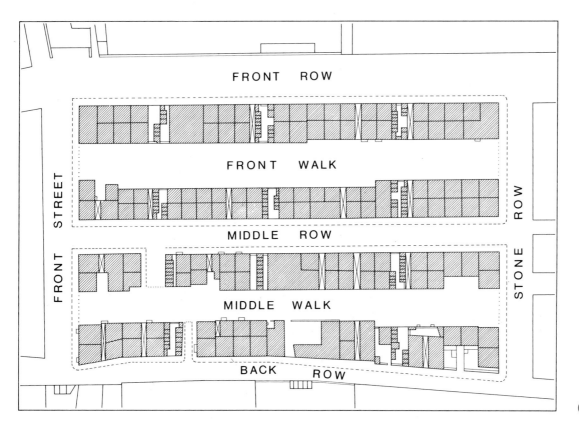

Fig 61.
The Camp Fields area
of Leeds:

(b) after improvement

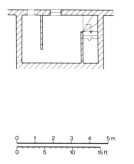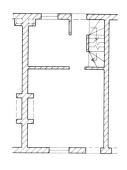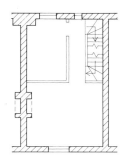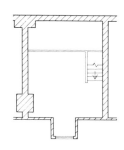

Fig 62. Council housing,
Derwent Avenue, Leeds

Plate 148.
Council housing,
Faxfleet Street, Bradford

Plate 149.
Council housing,
Draughton Street, Bradford

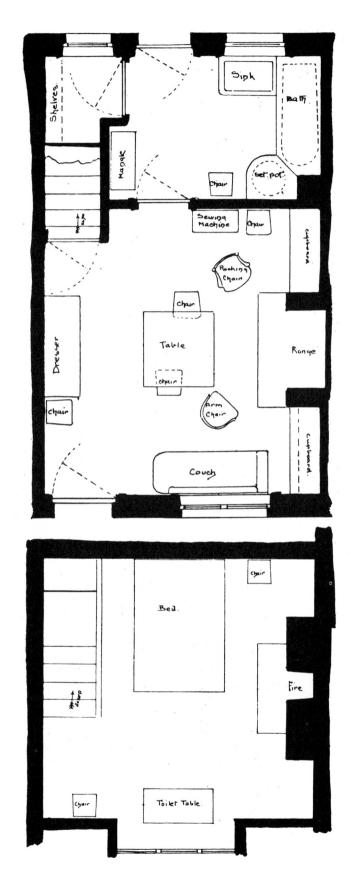

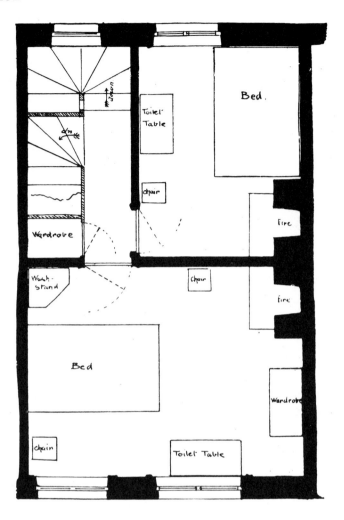

Plate 150 (*top left*).
Council housing, Faxfleet Street, Bradford:
original ground floor plan

Plate 151 (*top right*).
Council housing, Faxfleet Street, Bradford:
original first-floor plan

Plate 152 (*left*).
Council housing, Faxfleet Street, Bradford:
original attic plan

Plate 153.
Contemporary artist's
impression of Faxfleet Street
housing interiors: living room

Plate 154. Contemporary artist's impression of Faxfleet Street
housing interiors: first bedroom

Plate 155. Contemporary artist's impression of
Faxfleet Street housing interiors: scullery

Plate 156 (*right*).
Later council housing,
Faxfleet Street area,
Bradford

Plate 157 (*below*).
Later council housing,
Faxfleet Street area:
detail of porch

Being built of brick with tile roofs, rough-cast walls and façades relieved by a variety of decorative devices, they illustrate the latest developments in architectural design and have features which were to become characteristic of post-1919 council houses (Pls 156, 157).

In Huddersfield council houses built at this time followed more established designs (Pl 158), but at Normanton another departure from traditional building materials and practices is to be found in Haw Hill View. This row of houses was built in 1910 and, instead of forming part of a gridiron layout, was set facing a large green. Like the later Bradford houses, Haw Hill View was built of brick and tile, distinguished by decoratively used white bricks and canopies over the doors (Pls 159, 160).

Plate 158. Council housing, High Royd Crescent, Huddersfield

Plate 159 (*left*).
Council housing,
Haw Hill View,
Normanton

Plate 160 (*below*).
Council housing,
Haw Hill View,
Normanton: plans

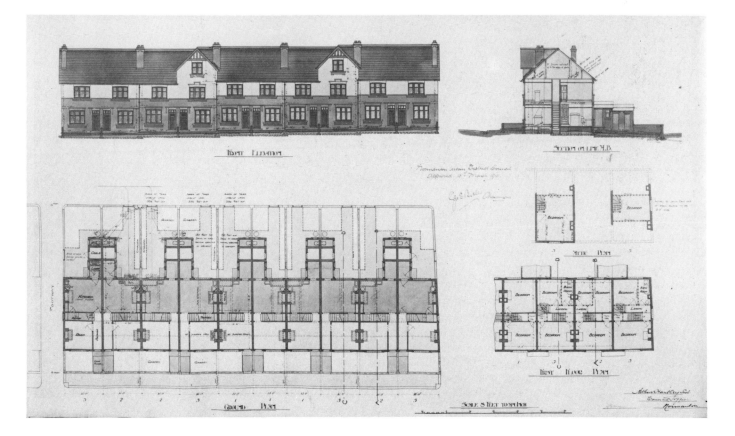

Plate 161 (*above*).
Woolman Street
(formerly Off Street)
council tenements, Leeds

Fig 63 (*right*)
Woolman Street
(formerly Off Street)
council tenements Leeds

BALCONY BALCONY

The high quality of the municipal housing at Normanton and Bradford may reflect a change in the local authorities' position as regards house-building and ownership. In 1919 the Housing and Town Planning Act abolished the stipulation, formerly in operation, that local authorities must sell within ten years any accommodation they built (Merrett 1979, 309). Subsequently, when they built houses, councils no longer had to provide dwellings that would appeal to potential purchasers. The houses remaining in council ownership acted, moreover, as a visible symbol of munificence and prestige, considerations which may have stimu-

lated the ostentation evident in the Haw Hill View and Faxfleet Street houses.

Prior to the 1919 Addison Act councils had to make their house-building schemes self-financing. In order to do so they charged comparatively high rents. Houses built by Huddersfield Corporation at Turnbridge between 1880 and 1882 were let for 3s 10d to 6s 3d a week (Balmforth 1918, 30), while those in Derwent Avenue, Leeds, carried a rent of 3s 9d to 4s 9d a week. The rent of the latter was twice reduced by 3d, but despite this the houses were not fully occupied until 1914 and even so it was a struggle for some to pay the rent. One woman stated that she had been able to afford to rent one of these houses only when her husband's wages were supplemented by those of her 13-year-old daughter (Leeds Housing Committee 1954, 13, 15). This being the case it may be wondered how many of the people displaced by clearance programmes actually took up places in the privately or corporation-built houses intended for their occupation. In an attempt to provide dwellings which such people could afford, the civic corporations began to investigate alternative forms of accommodation.

The type of housing which the corporations decided best met their requirements for cheap yet adequate accommodation was the tenemented block.[2] Although from this point of view the advantages of tenements had long been recognized (see p. 43), antipathy towards them had prevented their use in West Yorkshire in all but a very few cases. Speculators were not concerned to provide accommodation for the lowest paying tenants and so had no cause to adopt the tenement block, while most model builders preferred to provide cottage dwellings. Prospective occupants themselves disliked tenements. In 1906 Alderman Lupton stated that there was 'a strong preference on the part of . . . workmen for having a whole house to themselves and their families'. He pointed out further arguments against building tenements:

> land is easily attainable at a low price within a mile of the most crowded parts of the city, [so] that it is quite needless to introduce flats, or barracks as they are sometimes called, into Leeds, whilst there are objections to them on the score of want of privacy, as well as considerable difficulty in giving proper exercise to young children, who cannot come down from upper storeys in high buildings, and are therefore shut up in the dwellings whenever their mothers cannot look after them. The same objection applies when one considers the case of the old and infirm (Lupton 1906, 3).

Similar objections were raised in Huddersfield by the opponents of the Kirkgate tenement scheme (*Huddersfield Examiner* 21 December 1912).

Despite such objections, however, various corporations proceeded to build a number of tenement dwellings. By 1917 a third of Huddersfield's housing consisted of this type of accommodation (Balmforth 1918, 31). A survey made four years earlier of the occupants of the corporation's Moldgreen development showed that the policy of tenement building had succeeded in providing improved accommodation for a number of people at affordable rents. Of the thirty-eight tenements then in occupation twenty-two housed people who had formerly lived in condemned cellars. For the other tenants their new accommodation was an improvement on that which they had previously occu-

Plate 162. Woolman Street, Leeds: detail of tenements

pied, since four of them came from underdwellings and five from cellar dwellings not yet condemned (*Huddersfield Examiner*, 16 January 1913). The adoption of the tenement system introduced a new element into local authority housing, by attempting to provide accommodation for the least affluent members of society. It also involved implementing new methods of building and house design, plans adopted by the authorities frequently being ingenious and incorporating innovatory features.

The earliest extant tenements to be built in Leeds were constructed in 1901 in Woolman Street, originally Off Street (69). The block of thirty-nine tenements there was intended to rehouse 198 people displaced by the York Road clearance scheme (Pls 161, 162). Although it was actually built by private contractors, the plans were provided by the corporation along with the land on which it was to be constructed (Lupton 1906, 7). Each tenement contained a living-room, a scullery and either one or two bedrooms. A water closet and fuel store were situated on a rear balcony with access from the scullery (Fig 63). A few years later, in 1908, the council built another two blocks opposite, each containing twelve

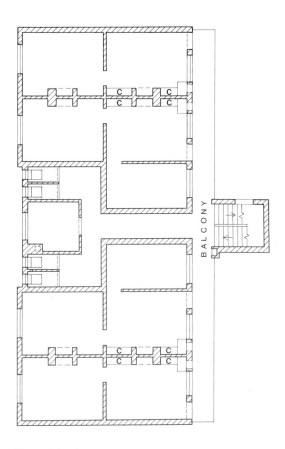

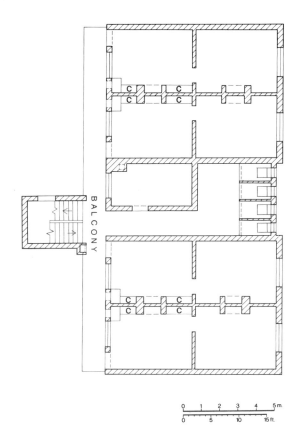

Fig 64 (*above*).
Marsh Lane Garth tenements, Marsh Lane, Leeds.
First-floor plans

Plate 163 (*right*).
Marsh Lane Garth council tenements, Leeds:
courtyard

flats but slightly different to each other in design (Marsh Lane Garth (68): Fig 64; Pls 163, 164). Again there was a mixture of one and two-bedroomed tenements but, unlike those in the Off Street block, the water closets were placed together and there was a communal washing-room on each floor. The ground-floor flats in these blocks had a shared ash-bin, while on the upper floors refuse was thrown into a chute which carried it down to an ash-hole below. To compensate for the lack of play-area and street space, land to the west of these tenements, formerly a graveyard, was left as open ground.

In Bradford the corporation completed their first tenement development in 1909. It consisted of five blocks, two of thirty flats and three of eighteen (30). It was built in the cleared Longlands Improvement Area and was intended to

Plate 164 (*left*).
Marsh Lane Garth
tenements, Leeds

Plate 165 (*below*).
Council tenements
in Longlands
Improvement Area,
Bradford

Plate 166 (*left*).
Council tenements in
Longlands Improvement
Area, Bradford

Plate 167 (*below*).
Council tenements
in Longlands
Improvement Area,
Bradford

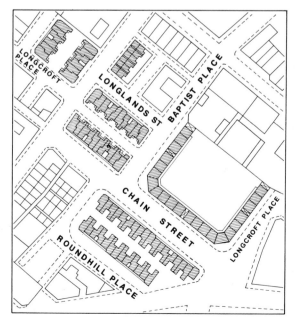

Plate 168 (*above*).
Council tenements in Longlands Improvement Area, Bradford

Fig 65 (*left*). Longlands Improvement Area, Bradford
(council housing hatched)

rehouse 432 displaced people (Brockway 1946, 52; Fig 65, Pls 165–8). The accommodation offered in these tenements and the way in which it was provided was very similar to the Off Street block in Leeds. Again each flat had a living-room, a scullery and one or two bedrooms, with a water closet and fuel store on a rear balcony. Stone, which had continued to be the main building material, was used for these blocks. The council appears to have been satisfied with them, for by 1910 they had built another two blocks of tenements on Chain Street and Roundhill Place (12). These were two-storeyed and contained single-roomed flats. A block of forty-eight tenements built in Huddersfield by J.F. Ramsden in 1911 was described as being 'similar' to these Bradford flats (*Huddersfield Examiner*, 8 February 1911).

Plate 169 (*left*).
Council tenements,
Mold Green, Huddersfield

Plate 170 (*right*).
Council tenements,
Kirkgate, Huddersfield

Plate 171 (*left*).
Council tenements,
Kirkgate, Huddersfield

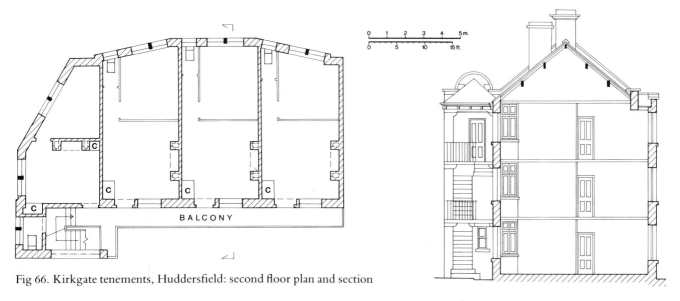

BALCONY

Fig 66. Kirkgate tenements, Huddersfield: second floor plan and section

The interest with which corporations and others followed the developments in neighbouring towns may well account for the similarities between designs. Following the success of their first four blocks of tenements built at Moldgreen in 1912–13 (Pl 169), Huddersfield Corporation embarked upon a further three blocks (60) in the Kirkgate Insanitary Area (Bamforth 1918, 31; Pls 170, 171; Fig 66). Before building these, members of the Corporation 'had visited Bradford two or three times and were copying what had been done

there' which, it was felt, 'had been such a great success' (*Huddersfield Examiner*, 18 December 1912, 16 January 1913). Similarities between the tenements built in different towns are not, therefore, unexpected, although these tend to be more in plan than in appearance. In some of their housing schemes it would appear that councils were over-ambitious. In Leeds the original plan for the Marsh Lane tenements was to provide one large block comprising forty-eight properties, similar in size and design to the Off Street block but

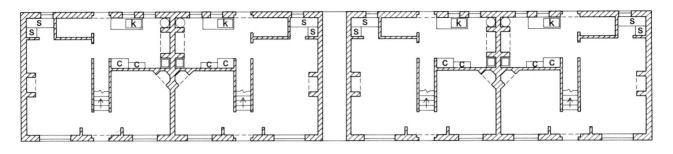

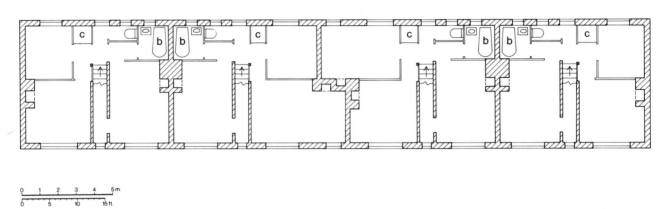

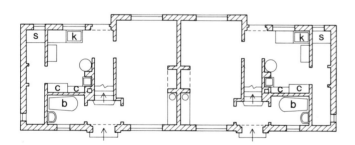

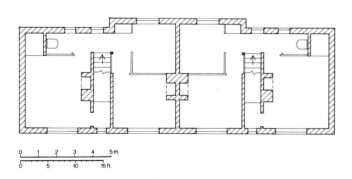

Fig 67. Council housing, Hawksworth, Leeds (1919)

with shops on the ground floor and various architectural embellishments. The plans for the building were drawn and passed the planning-approval stage, but before they were carried out the scheme had been reduced to the twenty-four flats which exist today (WYAS Leeds, Building Plan 20, 14 August 1903). Normanton Urban District Council's plans for Haw Hill View (95) were another example of a council having to modify its ideas. The original intention had been to make the terrace more architecturally decorative by using greater quantities of white brick and by breaking up the roof-line with dormer windows. The windows were intended to light attic bedrooms, but these were omitted when the houses were built, together with the bathrooms that had been designed in sixteen of the houses (John Goodchild Loan Collection: architect's plans of houses at Haw Hill Park, 1910; Pl 160).

The generous financial assistance provided by the Addison Act of 1919 enabled councils to spend more freely on the provision of housing. The average cost of a house built under its provisions was over £1,000, compared to a cost of £447 for a three-bedroomed, parlour house built in 1922 after the withdrawal of the 1919 subsidy (Leeds Housing Committee 1954, 15). The high cost of council housing built under the Addison Act was partly the result of keen competition for building labour and materials which pushed up prices. Not only did the act stimulate large council housing projects, but there was competition with private builders involved in the post-war industrial and commercial building boom (Walters 1927, 19).

High housing costs were also the result of developments in council housing policies. Following the trend of contemporary thought and the precepts given to them by central government, local authorities aimed to provide workers with accommodation of a higher standard than ever before. The reasoning behind this new attitude was two-fold. Firstly, the housing shortage had become so acute by the end of the First World War that it affected both well paid and less affluent workers alike. Housing policy planners felt that by building good-quality housing for the more affluent workers their former accommodation would be released for the less affluent, so improving standards of accommodation and reducing overcrowding for everyone (Finnigan 1980, 119). Secondly, it was believed that housing standards would continue to rise. In this case houses would have to be built to standards above the contemporary average in order to satisfy future requirements. If they did not do so it would then be difficult for the council to let the property and, therefore, it was felt to be worth spending more money than was strictly necessary at the time to ensure the future income from councils' houses (Walters' Report 1927, cited in Swenarton 1981, 94, 95).

The result of the new policy was the provision of large numbers of well built three-bedroomed houses, many of them containing a parlour as well as a living-room and scullery, and incorporating the latest architectural ideas on materials, design and layout (Swenarton 1981, 94–109, 144, 155; Fig 67). Unfortunately the theory which underlay the Addison Scheme was not proved in practice. Cheaper accommodation was not released for less affluent workers, since the new houses were frequently taken up by new family units as, for example, young couples who previously would have lived with a relative (Finnigan 1980, 114). Moreover, instead of the working man's ability to pay higher rents for improved accommodation increasing, as had been envisaged, the economic depression of the 1920s reversed the trend. Rents for the new houses, which in Leeds in 1919 ranged between 13s and 20s, compared unfavourably with that of 5s for a pre-1900 back-to-back, and put the council's houses beyond the reach of all but the most affluent skilled workers (Leeds Housing Committee 1954, 22–23). In 1922 the Medical Officer of Health had to conclude that the aims of the 1919 housing scheme had not been fulfilled:

> Unfortunately the new housing scheme affords no material assistance in solving the problem, because the high rentals of the new houses are beyond the means of the majority living in districts where most overcrowding exists (Leeds Housing Commitee 1954, 22).

In the light of this failure and of the financial demands of the subsidy the government, no longer faced with the threat of civil disorder, withdrew the Addison Act and its generous subsidy in 1921. Over the next two decades the nature of the councils' role as house-builders had to be redefined, along with reconsideration of the size and form which government housing subsidies should take (Leeds Housing Committee 1954, 22–23, 33; Merrett 1979, 310, 311; Finnigan 1980, 115–117, 121, 125, 138; Swenarton 1981, 144, 160, 161). It was, however, too late to remove local authorities from the ranks of house-builders, for standards and principles had been set which could not be abandoned easily. The local authorities had introduced new elements into the housing issue, both in attitudes and in building practice, and from the early 20th century they continued to play an important part in the provision of workers' housing.

Notes to Chapter 8
1 John Goodchild Loan Collection, County Medical Officer 1906, 343.
2 Councillor Thomas Burke of Bradford, who attended an international housing congress held in London in 1907, visited the newly developed Hampstead Garden Suburb. He reported that this housing, designed for the middle classes and for the better class of workmen 'did not interest one seeking information for Bradford, for insanitary area purposes'. He was more interested in a new type of tenement built in Camberwell (the maisonette), consisting of two-storeyed houses divided centrally and horizontally to provide four dwellings (WYAS, Bradford, Faxfleet Street housing box).

EPILOGUE

With the passing of the Addison Act in 1919 the government had clearly embarked on a policy of providing workers' housing, a policy which it has continued to pursue to the present day. The withdrawal of the Addison subsidy in 1921 proved to be only a temporary retraction from this commitment. Governmental concern over the issue of workers' housing continued and new subsidization schemes were soon introduced by the Chamberlain Act of 1923 and the Wheatley Act of 1924. These had as limited an effect in radically improving minimum living conditions as the Addison scheme. The subsidies of 1923 and 1924 were smaller than that of 1919, but it was not their reduced scale so much as the type of housing built with their aid that delayed improvement for the worst housed (Merrett 1979,

Plate 172. Quarry Hill flats, Leeds: aerial view

Plate 173.
Quarry Hill flats, Leeds:
general view

310–11). Although many municipal houses were built, their rents were still beyond the means of the lowest income groups, as too were the rents of any accommodation vacated by those who did move into local authority housing (Finnigan 1980, 117).

An important change in the direction of government housing policy came in 1930 with the introduction of a subsidy based on the number of people rehoused rather than on the number of houses built. The advantage of this approach was that local authorities began to concentrate their efforts on rehousing slum dwellers directly (Merrett 1979, 311). This policy was adopted in Leeds in 1933, where it was seen as being the first attempt yet made to deal with those underlying housing problems 'which had been a feature of urban life in Britain for over 100 years' (Finnigan 1980, 115). The council was faced with the problem of how to rehouse low-income families in accommodation of a sufficiently high standard, yet at rents which they could afford. The scale of the task called for a new approach. The council considered not only traditional solutions but also new ideas then being put into practice on the Continent. A working party was so impressed by the Austrian Republic's Karl Marx Hof flats in Vienna that it was decided to use them as a model for the projected Leeds development.

Between 1934 and 1940 a complex containing 938 flats was built in the Quarry Hill area of Leeds (Pls 172–5). These flats were built to accommodate over 3,000 people from the 'insanitary' housing which had previously occupied the site (Leeds Housing Committee 1938, 6). It was by this period government policy to encourage councils to build flats rather than houses because of their relatively low unit cost, without regard to the preferences of the prospective occupants. Conceptually Quarry Hill Flats represent an imported tradition, tenements being a long established urban housing type on the Continent, whereas in West Yorkshire individual houses were preferred. In most other respects, however, Quarry Hill represented a culmination of trends in the development of workers' housing over the previous two centuries.

The construction of these flats, a vast and expensive project, was financed with public money. That funds were now available for house building from this source and on such a scale was a significant development from the situation a century earlier, when money had been provided either by builders, employers, or small investors. In its day the largest house-building scheme undertaken in the county, Quarry Hill was, in a sense, a logical stage in the tendency to build increasingly larger housing developments.

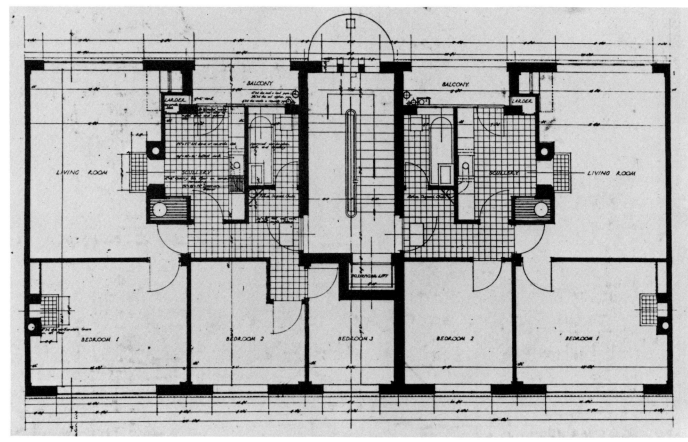

Plate 174. Quarry Hill flats, Leeds: plan of a pair of flats

The dwellings were designed in accordance with the most modern ideas as to accommodation, reflecting the extent to which standards had risen. A guide to the estate explained that

> Each dwelling contains an entrance hall, a living-room facing sunwards, a scullery leading on to a self-contained balcony also facing sunwards, a combined bathroom and w.c. which include a lavatory basin, 1–5 bedrooms, the first bedroom containing a built-in wardrobe and the second bedroom an angle clothes hanger.
>
> In addition there is a larder, a linen-cupboard, a combination of cupboards and drawers in the scullery, a china cupboard in the living-room and a fuel store (City of Leeds Housing Committee 1938, 9–10).

The flats were electrically lit and each contained a solid fuel cooking range which supplied hot water for the sink, bath and lavatory basin. Although this accommodation was not superior to much of that built by local authorities, the Quarry Hill scheme was important in raising the level of the minimum standard of housing.

A contemporary observer wrote with enthusiasm of modern flats in general and of Quarry Hill in particular:

> So many people continue to think of them as the old pre-war tenements, gloomy, stuffy, mechanical horrors, that they are completely frightened off the idea. But the best flats being built today are a thousand miles from that. To begin with, many are not merely blocks of flats. They are villages, as it were, with some dwellings on top of others. The most striking example in England, perhaps, is Quarry Hill, a block now being built in Leeds. This is to house over three thousand people. It is, in fact, a little town. It has its school . . . its communal hall and welfare centre, its shops, tennis-courts and bowling greens. There are to be four playgrounds with apparatus for children, an outside lavatory, wash-house, and so on – a complete social organism, with no gloomy courtyard and stagnant air. (Bertram 1938, 35).

He commended the 'new method of collecting refuse' by which it was 'thrown down the sink, old boots, tins, anything that will go in . . . though not old prams and

Plate 175. Quarry Hill flats, Leeds: detail showing construction

bedsteads'. The rubbish was then drawn by suction to incinerators where it was burned and the heat used for the wash-house, for 'from the moment a thing is thrown away it never appears again'. Other novel features were electric lifts and non-drip window boxes.

The materials and building methods used in the construction of Quarry Hill Flats marked a departure from the local building tradition. They were not built of brick because of the difficulty of manufacturing the quantity which the project would have required. Instead, they were built as a steel framework clad with concrete facing slabs, the first time that the method had been used in England (Nuttgens 1979, 55). This system, developed by a consortium of three local authorities, was a cheaper method of building than the traditional alternatives.

The concern of the model house builders of the mid 19th century that communal facilities, such as churches, schools, institutes and shops, should be provided for the residents of developments and that environmental considerations should also be taken into account, found expression at Quarry Hill. Although the flats provided high-density housing, they were built on only 18 per cent of the cleared slum area, the intention being to leave tracts of open ground around them (*ibid.*). The facilities provided in the complex included a laundry, a shopping centre, playgrounds and a day nursery. The planned social centre and sports area were, however, never built.

Quarry Hill Flats, incorporating as they did new ideas on housing and new methods of construction, represented a radically new solution to the problem of providing workers' housing on a large scale. Within thirty-five years of their construction, however, the development had been completely demolished and the council had moved on to experiment with other types of mass housing. Their demolition represented a failure of both the technology they incorporated and of the social experiment made possible by that technology.

INVENTORY

The selected monuments are arranged by alphabetical order of townships. All grid references (to eight figures unless referring to a large area of housing) are in 100 km square SE, except for numbers (49–52, 124, 131, 138–40 and 149) which are in square SD.

ADDINGHAM
(1) 10–20 Low Mill, Addingham (09104934).
(2) 23–31 Low Mill, Addingham (09084933).
(3) 10–16 and 36–42 The Rookery, Bolton Road, Addingham (07854984).

ALTOFTS
(4) 3–15 Co-operative Terrace, Lower Altofts, Normanton (38792446).

ARMLEY
(5) 153–159 Town Street, Armley, Leeds (26533351).

BEESTON
(6) 17 Noster Street, Beeston, Leeds (28903125).
(7) 20 Noster Street, Beeston, Leeds (28913124).

BINGLEY
(8) 2 and 3 Crowther Fold, Harden, Bingley (08593845).
(9) 17 and 19 Station Road, Cullingworth, Bingley (06633684).

BOLTON
(10) 1–40 Midland Terrace, Canal Road, Bradford (15983509).

BRADFORD
(11) 9–43 Baptist Place, 62–120 Chain Street and 1–35 Longcroft Place, Bradford (15893329).
(12) 1–71 Chain Street and 2–52 Roundhill Place, Bradford (15853325).
(13) 122–180 Chain Street and 121–179 Longlands Street, Bradford (15835333).
(14) 40–70 Southampton Street, Bradford (16963404).

BRAMLEY
(15) 2–6 and 42–44, 52–70 and 72–84 Coal Hill Lane, Farsley Beck Bottom, Leeds (22453545).

BURLEY IN WHARFEDALE
(16) 86–108 Main Street, Burley in Wharfedale, Ilkley (16514646).
(17) 8–30 Station Road, Burley in Wharfedale, Ilkley (16484637).

CARTWORTH
(18) Kenmore, Ryecroft, Ryecroft Lane, Holmfirth (15270740).
(19) Ryecroft Farm, Ryecroft Lane, Holmfirth (15240739).
(20) Sandy Gate Farm, Sandy Gate, Paris, Holmfirth (15470745).

CHAPEL ALLERTON
(21) 1–20 Husslers Row, Meanwood, Leeds (27963768).

CLAYTON
(22) 12–18 Back Lane, Off Highgate Road, Clayton (12093073).
(23) 2–6, 20–30 and 58–74 Highgate Road, Clayton (12113070).

CLAYTON WEST
(24) 30–48 Long Lane, Clayton West (25931142).

CLECKHEATON
(25) 4–8 Towngate, Scholes, Cleckheaton (16772589).

CRIGGLESTONE
(26) 1–18 and 19–40 Daw Green Avenue, Painthorpe, Crigglestone (31111576).
(27) 1–14 and 15–27 Garden Terrace, Painthorpe, Crigglestone (31051575).

CROFTON
(28) First Street to Seventh Street, New Crofton, Crofton (388174).

CUMBERWORTH HALF
(29) 13–23 Incumen Row, Skelmanthorpe (22801042).
(30) 11–19 Strike Lane, Skelmanthorpe (22941084).
(31) 10–28 Sunnyside Cottages, Crofthead, Skelmanthorpe (23281085).

DENBY
(32) 2–10 Dearneside Road, Denby Dale (22790837).

DEWSBURY
(33) 68–90 Thornhill Road, Dewsbury (23792075).
(34) 1–30 West Vale, Thornhill Road, Dewsbury (23772069).

ELLAND CUM GREETLAND
(35) Elland Wharfe, Elland (10692137).
(36) Elland Lock, Park Road, Elland (11102188).

FOULBY
(37) 1–47 Long Row, Nostell (40171662).

GARFORTH
(38) 1–4 Moor Cottages, Barwick Road, Garforth (40383373).

GILDERSOME
(39) 1 and 2 Burnt Side Road, Upper Moorside, New Farnley (24193056).
(40) 3–7 Moor Top, Upper Moorside, New Farnley (24163051).

GOLCAR
(41) 5–15 Wellhouse Fields, Upper Wellhouse, Golcar, Colne Valley (09481493).

HALIFAX
(42) West Hill Park, Halifax (085253).

HAREWOOD
(43) Harewood Village (322450).

HAWORTH
(44) 6–13 Lumbfoot, Stanbury, Keighley (01403744).

HEADINGLEY-CUM-BURLEY
(45) Lumley Mount, Leeds (27633507).
(46) William Street, Leeds (28323507).

HECKMONDWIKE
(47) 141–155 Union Street, Heckmondwike (21112334).

HEMSWORTH
(48) 52–104 Cow Lane, 1–55 and 2–40 East Street, 1–19 and 2–30 West Street, 1–37 and 2–42 South Street, and 1–45 and 2–44 Crescent Road, Havercroft, Hemsworth (39551425).

HEPTONSTALL
(49) 7–10 Northfield, Heptonstall (98732819).
(50) 1–8 Silver Street, Heptonstall (98572812).
(51) 2–22 Top o' the Town, Heptonstall (98622814).
(52) West Laithe, Heptonstall (98672800).

HESSLE
(53) Bar House, 9 Taylor Wood, Wragby, Hessle and Hill Top (41891677).

HONLEY
(54) Field End Farm, Honley, Holmfirth (14131157).
(55) 28 Oldfield, Holmfirth (13621028).
(56) 32 and 33 Oldfield, Holmfirth (13591028).
(57) 8–26 Upper Reins, Honley, Holmfirth (14081229).
(58) 1 and 2 St. Mary's Court, Honley, Holmfirth (13781207).

HUDDERSFIELD
(59) 1–39 Highroyd Crescent, Moldgreen, Huddersfield (15581647).
(60) First, Second and Third Blocks, Kirkgate Tenements, Kirkgate, Huddersfield (14731670).
(61) 1–39 and 2–36 Gelder Terrace, and 1–43 Poplar Street, Moldgreen, Huddersfield (Moldgreen Tenements) (15481623).
(62) 1–48 Ramsden's Tenements, Kirkgate, Huddersfield (14771665).
(63) 2–8 Wormald Yard, King Street, Huddersfield (14651657).

IDLE
(64) 25–31 Collier Row, Low Ash Road, Wrose, Idle (16083726).
(65) 50 and 52, Low Ash Road, Wrose, Idle (16133713).

KEIGHLEY
(66) 6–16 Goose Eye, Laycock, Keighley (02884062).

LEEDS
(67) Hollidays Court, Leeds (30503337).
(68) 1–24 Marsh Lane Garth, Marsh Lane, Leeds (30883339).
(69) 1–77 Woolman Street, Marsh Lane, Leeds (30853340).
(70) 1–4 Saint John's Court, Wade Lane, Leeds (30143387).
(71) Ship Yard, Briggate, Leeds (30203365).
(72) Turk's Head Yard, Briggate, Leeds (30193353).

LEPTON
(73) Bar Cottage, Rowley Lane, Lepton, Kirkburton (19551498).
(74) Ratten Row, 160–164 Wakefield Road, Lepton, Kirkburton (20561515).

LINGARDS
(75) 1–12 Holme Villas, Lingards Wood, Marsden (06321287).

LINTHWAITE
(76) 10–20 Barber Row, Linthwaite, Colne Valley (09531442).

(77) 437–445 Manchester Road, Linthwaite, Colne Valley (10561525).
(78) 467–483 Manchester Road, Linthwaite, Colne Valley (10491519).
(79) 52–76 Myrtle Grove, Linthwaite, Colne Valley (09501361).

LIVERSEDGE
(80) 134 Huddersfield Road, Heckmondwike (20222324).

LOCKWOOD
(81) 2–14 Quarry Road, Crossland Hill, Huddersfield (11601515).

LOTHERTON CUM ABERFORD
(82) 1–7 Bridge Cottages, Main Street, Aberford (43363726).
(83) 1 and 2 Bunkers Hill, Roman Road, Aberford (43343661).

MARSDEN
(84) Badger Hey, Meltham Road, Marsden, Colne Valley (06501225).
(85) 6–42 Derby Terrace, Brougham Road, Marsden, Colne Valley (09481163).
(86) Gilbert's Farm, Pule Hill, Marsden, Colne Valley (02841013).
(87) 1–4 and 17–23 Green Bower, Manchester Road, Marsden, Colne Valley (05261172).
(88) Redbrooke Engine House, Pule Hill, Marsden, Colne Valley (02541021).
(89) 1 and 2 ('Canalside') Tunnel End Cottages, Standedge, Marsden, Colne Valley (03961193).

MELTHAM
(90) 179–189 Huddersfield Road, Thongsbridge, Holmfirth (14500929).
(91) 1–29 and 2–32 Coniston Road, 1–9 Derwent Road and 1–9 Grasmere Road, Calmlands, Meltham (10251025).
(92) 35–59 St. Mary's Court, Wilshaw, Meltham (11820974).

MIDGLEY
(93) 1–5 Ewood Cottages, Midgley Road, Mytholmroyd, Halifax (02172641).

NORLAND
(94) 1–16 New Longley Lane, Norland, Sowerby Bridge (05352204).

NORMANTON
(95) 1–38 Haw Hill View, Normanton (39062314).

NORTH BIERLEY
(96) 39–51 Green End Road, Wibsey, North Bierley (14642990).
(97) 37–39 Hird Road, Low Moor, North Bierley (15732893).
(98) 15–26 Moor Top Road, Low Moor, North Bierley (14772894).
(99) 1–28 Railway Terrace, Low Moor, North Bierley (16522845).
(100) 7–10 School Fold, Low Moor, North Bierley (14912870).
(101) 1–7 Short Row, Low Moor, North Bierley (15732852).

NORTHOWRAM
(102) Akroydon, Boothtown Road, Halifax (089264).

OSSETT
(103) 41 Woodbine Street, Ossett (27962100).

OTLEY
(104) 51–97 Bradford Road, Otley (19644524).

OVENDEN
(105) 1–7 Club Houses, Ovenden, Halifax (07752749).

PUDSEY
(106) 3 Booths Yard, Lowtown, Pudsey (22373343).
(107) 3–6 Greenwood Row, Crimbles, Pudsey (22863334).

RAISTRICK
(108) Brookfoot Lock Cottage, Brighouse (13462279).

RAWDON
(109) Little London, Rawdon, Aireborough (204396).

SHARLSTON
(110) 1–46 Long Row, New Sharlston, Sharlston (38152039).

SHELF
(111) 7–17 Hudd Hill, Shelf, Queensbury and Shelf (11582799).
(112) 1–25 Springhead, Halifax Road, Shelf, Queensbury and Shelf (12142835).

SHIPLEY
(113) 2–26 Elliot Street and 2–26 Melbourne Street, Shipley (14093773).
(114) Saltaire, Shipley (138379).

SKIRCOAT
(115) Calder Terrace, Railway Terrace and St. Stephen's Street, Copley village, Halifax (08352255).
(116) Toll cottage, Copley Bridge, Copley, Halifax (08442231).

SOOTHILL
(117) 2–8 Broomsdale Road, Lower Soothill, Batley (25092404).

SOUTHOWRAM
(118) Salterhebble Lock House, Salterhebble Top Lock, Brighouse (09512245).
(119) 3–21 The Cottages, Marsh Lane, Halifax (10572455).

SOWERBY
(120) 2–18 Bethesda Row, Burnley Road, Mytholmroyd, Sowerby Bridge (00722637).
(121) 2–11 Bridge End, Burnley Road, Mytholmroyd, Sowerby Bridge (01212603).
(122) 7 and 9 Peter Row, Cragg Road, Sowerby Bridge (00602371).
(123) 5–16 Thorpe Place, Hubberton Green, Sowerby Bridge (03382286).
(124) 1–31 Victoria Buildings and 552–566 Halifax Road, Eastwood, Erringden (96302514).
(125) 11–33 Whitehouses, Burnley Road, Mytholmroyd, Sowerby Bridge (26250089).

STAINLAND
(126) 1–5 Croft Top, Outlane, Elland (08341782).

STANLEY-CUM-WRENTHORPE
(127) 160–182 Deputy Row, Potovens Lane, Outwood, Stanley (32452410).
(128) 1–7 Railway Terrace, off Lingwell Gate Lane, Outwood, Stanley (32512440).
(129) 3–13 Aire and Calder Cottages, Ward Lane, Stanley (35582286).
(130) Canal Cottage, Ramsdens Bridge, Ward Lane, Stanley (35502270).

STANSFIELD
(131) Rodwell End, Todmorden, Blackshaw (95732486).

THORPE
(132) Belmont Terrace and Ashfield Terrace, Thorpe, Lofthouse (31582652).

THORNTON
(133) 65 and 67 Back Heights Road, Moscow, Thornton (08883345).
(134) Half Acre, Close Head Row, Thornton (08543317).
(135) 8–22 Egypt, Thornton (09213401).
(136) 192–198 Hilltop Road, Thornton (09003316).
(137) 6–26 Long Row, Hill Top, Thornton (09363317).

TODMORDEN AND WALSDEN
(138) Churchill Street, Lydgate, Todmorden (92382551).
(139) Robinwood Terrace, Lydgate, Todmorden (92102552).
(140) Old Toll Bar, Rochdale Road, Steanor Bottom, Walsden, Todmorden (94521984).

TONG
(141) 89 Westgate Hill Street, Tong (29552085).

UPPER WHITLEY
(142) 1 Barnsley Road, Flockton, Kirkburton (22431512).
(143) 38 and 40 Briestfield Road, Grange Moor, Kirkburton (22181622).
(144) 1–4 Chapel Row, Briestfield Road, Grange Moor, Kirkburton (22141588).
(145) 1–4 Upper Row, Briestfield Road, Grange Moor, Kirkburton (22131600).
(146) 25–31 and 39–45 Wakefield Road, Grange Moor, Kirkburton (24141577).

WADSWORTH
(147) 1–7 Club Houses, Westfield, Old Town, Wadsworth (00092827).
(148) 1–6 Green End, Old Town, Wadsworth (00062810).
(149) Brunswick Street and Melbourne Street, Hebden Bridge, Hebden Royd (98902724).

WALTON
(150) Brooklands Avenue, Brooklands Road and Brooklands View, Walton (36011721).

WARLEY
(151) 1–5 Wainstalls Road, Wainstalls, Halifax (04652847).

WEST BRETTON
(152) 84–96 Brick Row, West Bretton (28581396).

WHITWOOD
(153) 1–19 Whitwood Terrace, Whitwood, Castleford (40502425).

WILSDEN
(154) Queen Street, Victoria Street, Albert Street, Wellington Street and Peel Street, Wilsden (09343593).
(155) 4–20 Club Row, Main Street, Wilsden (09273629).

WOOLDALE
(156) 21 and 23 Cinder Hills Road, Gully, Holmfirth (14670786).
(157) 124–130 Dunford Road, Holmfirth (14540775).

WYKE
(158) 1–5 Waterloo Fold, Wyke (15692684).

BIBLIOGRAPHY

PRINTED SOURCES CITED IN THE TEXT

ALDERSON, J.W. and OGDEN, A.E. (comps). 1921. *Jubilee 1871–1921* (Halifax).

ANDREAE, S. 1979. In M. Binney and D. Pearce (eds), *Railway Architecture* (London), 176–89.

BAKER, R. 1833. *Report of the Leeds Board of Health* (Leeds).

BAKER, R. 1842. Report on the condition of the residences of the labouring classes in the town of Leeds in the West Riding of York. *In Local reports on the sanitary condition of the labouring population of England* (London), 348–408.

BALMFORTH, O. 1918. *Jubilee History of the Corporation of Huddersfield, 1868–1918* (Huddersfield).

BARKE, M. 1975. Two industries in nineteenth-century Brighouse, *Trans. Halifax Antiq. Soc.* Dec. 1975, 93–6.

BERESFORD, M.W. 1971. The Back-to-Back House in Leeds, 1787–1837. *In* S.D. Chapman (ed.), *The History of Working-Class Housing: a Symposium* (Newton Abbot), 93–132.

BERESFORD, M.W. 1974. The Making of a Townscape: Richard Paley in the East End of Leeds, 1771–1803. *In* C.W. Chalklin and M.A. Havinden (eds), *Rural Change and Urban Growth 1500–1800* (London), 281–320.

BERESFORD, M.W. 1980. The face of Leeds, 1780–1914. *In* D. Fraser (ed.), *A History of Modern Leeds* (Manchester), 72–112.

BERTRAM, A. 1938. *Design* (Harmondsworth).

BODEY, H.A. 1971. Coffin Row, Linthwaite, *Ind. Archaeol.* viii, 381–91.

BRADFORD BENEFIT BUILDING SOCIETY. 1852. *Rules of the Bradford Benefit Building Society* (Bradford).

BRADFORD 1864. *Report of the Building and Improvement Committee on the operation of the building bye-laws* (Bradford).

BRADFORD 1865. *Bye-laws made by the Council of the Borough of Bradford* (Bradford).

BRADFORD 1870. *Bye-laws for the regulation of new streets and building within the Borough of Bradford* (Bradford).

BRADFORD 1875. *Borough of Bradford. Building Regulations* (Bradford).

BRADFORD 1897. *City of Bradford. Building Regulations* (Bradford).

BRADFORD 1904. *Faxfleet Street Workmen's Dwellings. Description and Plans with some suggestions as to furnishings* (Bradford).

BRADFORD SANITARY COMMITTEE. 1845. *Report of the Bradford Sanitary Committee* (Bradford).

BRETTON, R. 1948. Colonel Edward Akroyd, *Trans. Halifax Antiq. Soc.* June 1948, 60–100.

BROCKWAY, F. 1946. *Socialism over sixty years* (London).

BROWN, R. 1799. *General view of the Agriculture of the West Riding of Yorkshire* (Edinburgh).

CALDWELL, J. 1899. *History of Brighouse and its Co-operative Society* (Brighouse).

CHALKLIN, C.W. 1974. *The Provincial Towns of Georgian England: a study of the building process, 1740–1820* (London).

CLEGG, C. 1915. Turnpikes and toll-bars, *Trans. Halifax Antiq. Soc.*, 325–57

CORNES, J. 1905. *Modern housing in town and country* (London).

CUDWORTH, W. 1891. *Histories of Bolton and Bowling* (Bradford).

CUDWORTH, W. 1977. *Condition of the industrial classes of Bradford and District* (Queensbury).

CUNNINGTON, P. 1980. *How old is your house?* (Sherbourne).

CUTLER, T.W. 1896. *Cottage and country buildings* (London).

DAUNTON, M.J. 1983. *House and Home in the Victorian City: Working Class Housing 1850–1914* (London).

DEFOE, D. 1971. *A Tour through the Whole Island of Great Britain* (Harmondsworth), first pub. 1724–6.

DEWHIRST, R.K. 1960–61. Saltaire, *Town Plan. Rev.* xxxi, 135–44.

DODSWORTH, C. 1971. The Low Moor ironworks, Bradford, *Ind. Archaeol.* viii, 122–64.

FACER, P. and GASSE, I. 1980. The people's friend?, *Pennine Heritage* May, 17–19.

FINNIGAN, R. 1980. Housing policy in Leeds between the wars. *In* J. Melling (ed.), *Housing, Social Policy and the State* (London).

GASKELL, S.M. 1971. Yorkshire estate development and the freehold land societies in the nineteenth century, *Yorkshire Archaeol. J.* xliii, 158–65.

GASKELL, S.M. 1983. *Building Control: National Legislation and the Introduction of Local Bye-Laws in Victorian England* (London).

GAULDIE, E. 1974. *Cruel Habitations: A History of Working-Class Housing 1780–1918* (London).

GOODCHILD, J. 1961. *West Riding turnpike trusts– a list* (Wakefield).

GOODCHILD, J. 1975. *Normanton town trail* (Wakefield).

GOODCHILD, J. 1976. *Coalmining at Sharlston, an historical essay* (Wakefield).

GOODCHILD, J. 1977. *Pope and Pearson and Silkstone Building, the origins of a West Riding colliery and colliery community* (Wakefield).

GOODCHILD, J. 1978. *The Coal Kings of Yorkshire* (Wakefield).

HAIGH, A. 1978. *Railways in West Yorkshire* (Clapham), 2nd ed.

HALIFAX 1850. *Bye-laws passed by the Council of the Borough of Halifax 1849* (Halifax).

HALIFAX 1869. *Copy of bye-laws and portions of Acts of Parliament in force within the Borough with regard to streets and buildings* (Halifax).

HALIFAX 1893. *Bye-laws and portions of Acts of Parliament with regard to new streets and buildings* (Halifax).

HOBSON, O.R. 1953. *A Hundred years of the Halifax* (London).

HOLE, J. 1866. *Homes of the Working Classes with Suggestions for their Improvement* (London).

HOLMES, D.H. 1967. *The mining and quarrying industries in the Huddersfield district* (Huddersfield).

IDLE 1864. *Bye-laws for the district of Idle* (Bradford).

JEWELL, J. 1819. *The tourist's companion or the history and antiquities of Harewood in Yorkshire . . .* (Leeds).

KELLY & CO. 1893. *Kelly's Directory of the West Riding of Yorkshire* (London).

KUSSMAUL, A. 1981. *Servants in husbandry in early modern England* (Cambridge).

LEEDS 1838. *Bye-laws passed by the Council of the Borough of Leeds* (Leeds).

LEEDS 1842. *Bye-laws passed by the Council of the Borough of Leeds* (Leeds).

LEEDS 1870. *Bye-laws with sections of acts relating to new streets, building, etc.* (Leeds).

LEEDS 1878. *Extracts from acts in force in Leeds relating to streets and buildings etc.* (Leeds).

LEEDS 1901. *Leeds Local Acts, 1842–1901* (Leeds).

LEEDS (City of), Housing Committee. 1938. *Quarry Hill Flats* (Leeds).

LEEDS (City of), Housing Committee. 1954. *A short history of civic housing* (Leeds).

LEEDS Permanent Building Society. 1948. *A survey of one hundred years: Leeds Permanent Building Society 1848–1948* (Leeds).

LEWIS, B. 1971. *Coal mining in the eighteenth and nineteenth centuries* (London).

LINSTRUM, D. and POWELL, K. 1977. *Victorian Society Anglo–American study Tour, 26 June* (Leeds).

LOUDON, J.C. 1840. *An Encyclopaedia of Cottage, Farm, and Villa Architecture and furniture* (London).

LOWE, J.B. 1977. *Welsh Industrial Workers' housing 1775–1875* (Cardiff).

LUMB, F.E. 1951. *Second thoughts. A history of the Bradford Equitable Building Society* (Bradford and London).

LUPTON, F.M. 1906. *Housing improvements: a summary of ten years' work in Leeds* (Leeds).

MAIR, L.W.D. 1910. *Local Government Board report on back-to-back houses* (London).

MAWSON, R. and HUDSON, R. 1893. *Report as to the best mode of building cottages* (Bradford).

MEE, G. 1975. *Aristocratic enterprise: the Fitzwilliam Industrial Undertakings 1795–1857* (Glasgow and London).

MERRETT, S. 1979. *State housing in Britain* (London).

MORRIS, C. (ed.) 1947. *The Journeys of Celia Fiennes* (London).

MUTHESIUS, S. 1982. *The English terraced house* (Newhaven and London).

NORMAN, W.L. 1969. Fall Ings, Wakefield: some notes on an 18th-century foundry, *Ind. Archaeol.* vi, 74–79.

NUTTGENS, P. 1979. *Leeds. The back to front, inside out, upside down city* (Otley).

ORBACH, L. 1977. *Homes fit for heroes. A study of the evolution of British public housing 1915–1921.*

PARLIAMENTARY PAPERS 1806. *Report from the Committee on the state of the woollen manufacture of England* (London).

PARLIAMENTARY PAPERS 1842. *Report of the Commissioners into the employment of children in mines* (London).

PARLIAMENTARY PAPERS 1885. *Royal Commission on the housing of the working classes. Minutes and Evidence. First Report, 1884–5* (London).

PEVSNER, N. 1943. Model houses for the labouring classes, *Architectural Review* xciii, 119–28.

PRIESTLEY, J. 1831. *Historical account of the navigable rivers, canals and railways, throughout Great Britain, as a reference to Nichols, Priestley and Walker's new map of inland navigation* (London and Wakefield).

PUBLIC GENERAL STATUTES 1868. *A collection of the public general statutes passed in the thirty-first and thirty-second years of the reign of Her Majesty Queen Victoria, 1867–8* (London).

PUBLIC GENERAL STATUTES 1847. *A collection of the public general statutes passed in the tenth and eleventh year of the reign of Her Majesty Queen Victoria, 1847* (London).

PUBLIC GENERAL STATUTES 1875. *The public general statutes passed in the thirty-eighth and thirty-ninth years of the reign of Her Majesty Queen Victoria, 1875* (London).

PYE, D. 1981. *The Housing of the Working Classes Act, 1890, and the Longlands Insanitary Area* (Bradford).

RCHM, forthcoming. *Rural houses of West Yorkshire, 1400–1830* (London).

REYNOLDS, J. 1983. *The Great Paternalist: Titus Salt and the Growth of Nineteenth-Century Bradford* (Bradford).

RIMMER, W.G. 1955. Middleton Colliery, near Leeds (1770–1830), *Yorkshire Bull. Econ. Soc. Res.* vii. 40–57.

RIMMER, W.G. 1963. Working Men's Cottages in Leeds, 1770–1840, *Publ. Thoresby Soc.* xlvi, 165–99.

RIMMER, W.G. 1963. Alfred Place Terminating Building Society, 1825–1843, *Publ. Thoresby Soc.* xlvi, 303–30.

ROWNTREE, B.S. and PIGOU, A.C. 1914. *Lectures on housing* (Manchester).

SCATCHERD, N. 1874. *The History of Morley*, 2nd ed. (Morley).

SCHOFIELD, R.B. 1981. The construction of the Huddersfield Narrow Canal, 1794–1811, *Trans., Newcomen Soc.* liv, 17–38.

SHEERAN, G. 1984. *Aire Valley vernacular architecture.*

SIMPSON, D. 1979. *C.F.A. Voysey, an architect of individuality* (London).

SMITH, W. 1866. *Rambles about Morley* (London).

STELL, C.F. 1965. Pennine Houses: An Introduction, *Folk Life* iii, 5–24.

SYMONDS, J. 1976. *Catalogue of the drawings collection at the Royal Institute of British Architects: C.F.A. Voysey* (London).

SWENARTON, M. 1981. *Homes Fit for Heroes. The politics and architecture of early state housing in Britain* (London).

TARN, J.N. 1973. *Five per cent Philanthropy. An Account of Housing in Urban Areas 1840–1914* (Cambridge).

TAYLOR, K. 1978. *Wakefield District Heritage* (Wakefield).

THOMPSON, B. 1982. Public provision and private neglect: public health. *In* D.G. Wright and J.A. Jowitt (eds), *Victorian Bradford* (Bradford), 137–64.

THOMPSON, E.P. 1980. *The Making of the English Working Class* (Harmondsworth, first pub. 1963).

THORNES, R.C.N. 1981. *West Yorkshire: 'A Noble Scene of Industry'. The Development of the County 1500 to 1830* (Wakefield).

WALTERS, J.T. 1927. *The Building of Twelve Thousand Houses* (London).

WARD, J.T. 1970. *The factory system* (Newton Abbot).

WEBSTER, E. 1978. Halifax in 1851, *Halifax Antiq. Soc. Papers* 1976–79, October, 42–53.

WEST YORKSHIRE (Metropolitan County Council) forthcoming. *West Yorkshire Towns: their history and development* (Wakefield).

WILDING, D. 1977. *From Scales to Scholes* (Cleckheaton).

WILSON, R.G. 1971. *Gentlemen Merchants: The merchant community in Leeds 1700–1830* (Manchester).

UNPUBLISHED AND MANUSCRIPT SOURCES

BRITISH WATERWAYS BOARD. Commissioners' plan of the Aire and Calder Navigation, 1775.

BRITISH WATERWAYS BOARD. Plan of the Calder and Hebble Navigation drawn (? 1834) from a survey taken in 1806.

BROWN, W. 1821. *Information regarding flax spinning at Leeds*, typed copy held at Leeds City Reference Library.

Cellar Clough Mills, Marsden. Papers held by.

Deeds held by owner of 11 Thorpe Place, Hubberton Green, Sowerby.

GELDART, J.R. 1975. 'The changing conditions of working-class housing in Bradford 1870–1970', typescript held at Bradford Central Library, Local Studies Department.

GLOVER, F.J. 1959. 'Dewsbury Mills', unpublished Ph D. thesis, University of Leeds.

HALIFAX BUILDING SOCIETY. Correspondence concerning the competition for designs of model cottages for West Hill Park, 1863.

HALIFAX BUILDING SOCIETY. General Ledger, 1897–1913.

HALIFAX BUILDING SOCIETY. North Bierley Equitable Benefit Building Society: rough minute book (starting October 1876).

HALIFAX BUILDING SOCIETY. Hume, R. 1931. 'History of Loyal Georgians' – a paper given before members of the Halifax Rotary Club, photocopy of typescript.

JOHN GOODCHILD LOAN COLLECTION (JGLC). County Medical Officer 1903. *The sanitary surveys of the West Riding poor law unions.* Vol. i (Wakefield).

JOHN GOODCHILD LOAN COLLECTION. County Medical Officer 1906. *Report of the county medical officer upon the sanitary condition of the Wakefield Rural District* (Wakefield).

JOHN GOODCHILD LOAN COLLECTION. Architect's drawings of houses built for Normanton District Council at Haw Hill Park, 1910.

KIRKLEES LIBRARIES, Local Studies Department. Huddersfield Corporation scrapbook (containing newspaper cuttings).

KIRKLEES LIBRARIES, Local Studies Department. *Huddersfield Daily Examiner*, 1911 (on microfilm).

LEEDS CITY REFERENCE LIBRARY. Leeds City Council Engineer's Department, 1901. Photographs of Unhealthy Areas (five volumes).

LEEDS PERMANENT BUILDING SOCIETY (LPBS). Surveyors' Book, 1851–2; Surveyors' Field Book, no. 10, 1900.

MYERS, C.M.H. 1971. 'Low Moor, the story of a village', unpublished typescript (copy used belongs to Mrs Briggs, 10 School Fold, Low Moor).

PUBLIC RECORD OFFICE (PRO). RAIL 236/286/14; RAIL 491/360; RAIL 527/952; RAIL 527/1145.

STELL, C.F. 1960. 'Vernacular architecture in a Pennine community', unpublished M.A. thesis, Liverpool University.

Survey (of Harewood) 1796 *see* WYAS Ls.

UNIVERSITY OF LEEDS, Brotherton Library. MS 160 (Henry Briggs Son & Co. Ltd., Minute Book 1, 1865–82).

West Hill Park Competition 1863 *see* HALIFAX BUILDING SOCIETY.

WEST YORKSHIRE ARCHIVE SERVICE, Bradford (WYAS, Bf.). Building Plans.

WYAS, Bf. Building Plans Index.

WYAS, Bf. Faxfleet Street Papers.

WYAS, Bf. MSC/33 (Low Moor Ironworks Company stock books, 1795–1835).

WYAS, Bf. WE Preston Papers, box 7, 7/1 a–e (manorial court records).

WEST YORKSHIRE ARCHIVE SERVICE, Calderdale (WYAS, Cal.). HXM: 296, 297, 299 (Halifax Corporation Health and Sanitary Committee Minute Books, vol. i, 1848–53; vol. ii, 1853–57; vol. iv, 1865–71).

WYAS, Cal. HXM: 419, 420 (Halifax Corporation Health and Sanitary Committee report books, no. i, 1849–54; no. 2, 1854–77).

WYAS, Cal. HXM: 157, 158, 162 (Halifax Corporation Improvement Committee minute books, vol. ii, 1854–8; vol. iii, 1858–65; vol. vii, 1882–88).

WEST YORKSHIRE ARCHIVE SERVICE, Headquarters (WYAS, HQ). English, B.A. 1965. *Handlist of West Riding Enclosure Awards.*

WYAS, HQ. RT31 (Huddersfield and New Hey Turnpike Road papers).

WYAS, HQ. RT42 (Huddersfield and Penistone Turnpike Road papers).

WYAS, HQ. RT94 (Wakefield and Halifax Turnpike Trust: contract for turnpike house at Smith Lane End, 1805).

WEST YORKSHIRE ARCHIVE SERVICE, Kirkless (WYAS Kirk). Whitley Beaumont Estate Papers 153 (Survey of Little Lepton 1822); 1/22 (accounts for repair of cottages at Kirkheaton, 1749).

WYAS Kirk. BTC 912 1634 (Senior Map of Almondbury, 1934).

West Yorkshire Archive Service, Leeds (WYAS Ls). Building Plans

WYAS Ls. Building Plans Index.

WYAS Ls. Buckle, W.H. 1975. 'Harewood (a guide for the information of schools)', typescript.

WYAS Ls. Harewood Survey, 1796. No. 64, part 1.

WEST YORKSHIRE ARCHIVE SERVICE, Wakefield (WYAS Wf). Censuses for Hubberton Green, Sowerby, 1841; Lepton, 1841; Lingards, 1871; Shelf, North Bierley, 1851; Wyke, North Bierley, 1861.

YORKSHIRE ARCHAEOLOGICAL SOCIETY. DD146 (Plan of Baildon Common, 1610); DD174 (Map of Silsden, Braithwaite Gill Grange and area).

OTHER WORKS CONSULTED

ARMITAGE, H. no date. *'Dawson City', Heptonstall.*

ARMITAGE, H. 1977. 'Dam it! – the building of Halifax reservoirs 1830–1914, *Halifax Antiq. Papers*, 1976–9, February, 1–21.

ATKINSON, F. 1965. Yorkshire miners' cottages, *Folk Life* iii, 9–26.

BAIN, J. (ed.). 1939. *The authentic map directory of south-west Yorkshire* (London).

BARKE, M. 1979. Weavers' cottages in the Huddersfield area: a preliminary survey, *Folk Life* xvii, 49–59.

BERBIERS, J.L. 1968. The Victorian working-class homes of Halifax, *Municipal Review* xxxix, 24–5.

BINNEY, M. 1979. Land of the yeoman clothier. The Colne Valley, West Yorkshire, *Country Life* cxlv, 2362–4.

BODEY, H.A. 1972. *Industrial history in Huddersfield* (Huddersfield).

BOWTELL, H.D. 1979. *Reservoir railways of the Yorkshire Pennines* (Blandford).

BRADFORD IMPROVED COMMERCIAL BUILDING SOCIETY. 1838. *Articles, rules and regulations of a building society* (Bradford).

BRADFORD THIRD EQUITABLE BENEFIT BUILDING SOCIETY. 1856. *Rules and tables of the Bradford Third Equitable Benefit Building Society* (Bradford).

BREAKELL, B. 1982. *People who make the Pennines* (Hebden Bridge).

BROCKLEHURST, W.H. 1906. *A record of the origins and progress of Low Moor ironworks from 1791 to 1906* (Bradford).

BURNETT, J. 1978. *A Social History of Housing 1815–1970* (Newton Abbot).

COUNTY MEDICAL OFFICER. 1966. *Report of the County Medical Officer upon the Sanitary condition of the Wakefield Rural District* (Wakefield).

DARLEY, G. 1975. *Villages of vision* (London).

DAVIS, W. 1971. *Hints to philanthropists, or a collective view of practical means for improving the condition of the poor and labouring classes of society* (Shannon). First edition 1821 (Bath).

DOUGLAS, J. 1980. Early 19th-century working-class housing in Leeds, *Victorian Soc. West Yorkshire Group Journ.*, 10–12.

FIRTH, G. 1977. The origins of Low Moor Ironworks, Bradford, 1788–1900, *Yorkshire Archaeol. J.* xlix, 127–39.

HARWOOD, H.W. 1968. As things were. A social study of the Upper Calder Valley, *Trans. Halifax Antiq. Soc.*, 15–25.

HOBSBAWM E.J. 1974. *Industry and Empire* (Harmondsworth).

HOLROYDE, H. 1979. Textile mills, masters and men in the Halifax district, 1770–1851, *Halifax Antiq. Soc. Papers 1976–9*, 57–79.

IDLE 1894. *Bye-laws for the district of Idle* (Bradford).

JAGGER, M. 1914. *The history of Honley* (Huddersfield).

JENKINS, D.T. 1975. *The West Riding wool textile industry 1770–1835. A study of fixed capital formation* (Edington).

JOY, D. 1975. *A regional history of the railways of Great Britain: vol. 38, South and West Yorkshire* (London).

LINSTRUM, D. 1978. *West Yorkshire, Architects and Architecture* (London).

LOWE, H. 1968. The Bowling Ironworks, *Ind. Archaeol.* v, 171–77.

MICHELMORE, D.J.H. 1972. The domestic vernacular architecture of the Holme Valley 1750–1939 – an outline, *Brigantian* i, 10–11.

NEILL, A. 1873. On the Bradford building trades, *Report of the forty-third meeting of the British Association for the Advancement of Science*, 196–99.

NEWTON, G.D. 1976. Single-storey cottages in West Yorkshire, *Folk Life* xiv, 65–74.

PEARCE, C. 1980. A model example, *Pennine Magazine* i, no. 2, 20–21.

PEARCE, C. 1980. A community sewn up, *Pennine Magazine* i, no. 5, 20–21.

POLLARD, S. 1964. The factory village in the Industrial Revolution, *Engl. Hist. Rev.* lxxix, 513–31.

PRICE, S.J. 1958. *Building Societies, their origin and history* (London).

RAVETZ, A. 1971. The history of a housing estate, *New Society*, 907–10.

RAVETZ, A. 1974. *Model estate: planned housing at Quarry Hill, Leeds.*

SANDWITH, H. 1843. *Two lectures on the defective arrangements in large towns to secure the health and comfort of their inhabitants* (London).

SHANNON, H.A. 1934. Bricks – a trade index, 1785–1849, *Economica*, new series, i, 300–18.

SMITH, W.J. 1977. The cost of building Lancashire loomhouses and weavers' workshop: the account book of James Brandwood of Turnton, 1794–1814, *Textile History* viii, 56–76.

SUTCLIFFE, A. 1972. Working-class housing in 19th-century Britain: a review of recent research, *Bulletin, Soc. for Study of Labour Hist.* xxiv, 40–51.

TAYLOR, R.F. 1966. A type hand-loom weaving cottage in mid-Lancashire, *Ind. Archaeol.* iii, 251–5.

TIMMINS, G. 1982. Towards a procedure for recording threatened buildings, *Local Hist.* xv, 6–20.

WIGHTMAN, W. 1880. How I joined a building club, *Bradford Observer*, 24 Dec.

INDEX